Experiencing GOD®

Around The Kitchen Table

LIFE LESSONS FROM

Marilynn Blackaby

with Carrie Blackaby Webb

Experiencing God Around the Kitchen Table
Copyright © 2008 by Marilynn Blackaby and Carrie Blackaby Webb
All rights reserved. International copyright secured.

A Focus on the Family book published by
Tyndale House Publishers, Inc., Carol Stream, Illinois 60188

Focus on the Family and the accompanying logo and design are trademarks of Focus on the Family, Colorado Springs, CO 80995.

TYNDALE and Tyndale's quill logo are registered trademarks of Tyndale House Publishers, Inc.

EXPERIENCING GOD® is a registered trademark of LifeWay Christian Resources, Nashville, TN.

Focus on the Family gratefully acknowledges permission from LifeWay Christian Resources to use the trademarked phrase EXPERIENCING GOD® in the title of this book.

The authors are represented by the literary agency of Wolgemuth & Associates.

All Scripture quotations, unless otherwise indicated, are taken from the New King James Version®. Copyright © 1982 by Thomas Nelson, Inc. Used by permission. All rights reserved.

Scripture quotations marked (AMP) are taken from The Amplified Bible, Old Testament. Copyright © 1965, 1987 by the Zondervan Corporation. The Amplified New Testament, copyright © 1954, 1958, 1987 by the Lockman Foundation. Used by permission. (www.Lockman.org).

Editor: Kathy Davis
Cover design by: Joseph Sapulich
Cover photograph of flower copyright © by Selahattin Bayram/iStockphoto. All rights reserved.
Cover photograph of floral frame copyright © by Evgeniy Ivanov/iStockphoto. All rights reserved.
Cover photograph of old framed paper copyright © by Peter Zelei/iStockphoto. All rights reserved.
Author photographs by Pro Studio at the Garden Cottage, McDonough, GA. Copyright ©
Marilynn Blackaby; Copyright © Carrie Blackaby Webb.

Library of Congress Cataloging-in-Publication Data
Blackaby, Marilynn.
  Experiencing God around the kitchen table / Marilynn Blackaby and Carrie Blackaby Webb.
    p. cm.
  Includes bibliographical references.
  ISBN-13: 978-1-58997-469-2
  ISBN-10: 1-58997-469-7
  1. Mothers—Religious life. 2. Wives—Religious life. 3. Family—Religious aspects—
Christianity. I. Webb, Carrie Blackaby. II. Title.
  BV4529.18.B4755 2008
  248.8′431—dc22

                    2008016208

Printed in the United States of America
1 2 3 4 5 6 7 8 9 / 14 13 12 11 10 09 08

From Marilynn
I have experienced different seasons in my life: growing up in the
family home, marriage and children, and life after the children
are grown. I would like to dedicate this book to my parents,
Melvin and Carrie Wells. They gave me a strong foundation
in the first season of my life, which helped me experience all the
joys and success that later would come as I walked with the Lord.

From Carrie
I would like to dedicate this book to my two children,
Elizabeth and Joshua, with the prayers that I can be the
same example that my mother was for me.

CONTENTS

FOREWORD

Experiencing God Around the Kitchen Table could easily be called *A Mother and Wife's Testimony to the Faithfulness of God.* Throughout the pages of this book, Marilynn is transparent and honest about her life as a mother and wife: her pain, her fears, her joys and tears, her expectations and their fulfillment, and her daily trust in the faithfulness of God.

As her husband, I can bear witness to her unwavering trust in God. Though often tested in her faith, she never failed to trust Him for His wisdom, goodness, and provision.

This book contains an honest and timely look back at a lifetime of struggle and pain. But through it all, Marilynn was always a happy person who was overflowing with much laughter and joy. Her music—at the piano, singing—always filled the house (and often the neighborhood) with music. Her gift of song brought delight to those around her and continues to do so even to this day.

As I read this manuscript, I learned a lot about my wonderful wife of 47 years. Although we went through many of these experiences together, it was very inspiring and humbling to see these events through the eyes of my wife. I know that this book will encourage many women as they identify with her life and her experiences.

To me, Marilynn's life is a clear example of God's promises, especially 1 Samuel 2:30: "Those who honor Me, I will honor." She sought at all times to honor God. From the time she was a little girl, honoring her Lord was, and continues to be, the passion of her life. This passion led her to be involved in all the mission organizations of her church, especially in her college years. Because of this, she has always brought a heart for missions to our marriage. So we both, with one heart, have laid our lives, our marriage, and our children before God for His eternal purposes.

Is it any wonder that this resulted in our home having an atmosphere in which God could call all five of our children into some form of ministry? All five are, to this day, in full-time ministry. In our marriage, we have never struggled with any call or assignment from God in missions. Even in our "retirement years," we are overwhelmed by all God continues to let us do around the world.

Marilynn continues to be a godly helpmate, as God designed her to be (Genesis 2:18). She is a helper not only to her family but to almost everyone she meets—especially in her church and neighborhood. She is an amazing person shaped by God (Ephesians 2:19–22). Her life is also a picture of the virtuous woman, fully described in Proverbs 31:10–31. She is always working with her hands, sewing, knitting, and making things for her family, missionaries, and the needy around her. And Proverbs 31:28 is her reward: "Her children rise up and call her blessed; her husband also, and he praises her."

We welcome you to our home, around our kitchen table, to hear the stories of God's faithfulness.

—HENRY T. BLACKABY

INTRODUCTION

Throughout the years, God has allowed me to encounter many lives and share with others about the Lord. After hearing about what God has done in our lives, people are often interested in how we were able to remain faithful through all the different hardships and challenges and to complete all that God has led us to do. Many have told me that I need to write these stories down so that others can be encouraged by seeing God's faithfulness. After so many years, I feel that God does want me to share some of what He has taught me through my experiences with Him.

My main purpose in writing this for you is to encourage you to know God and to trust Him, to be obedient, and to learn how faithful He is. You are not alone in your struggles, nor do you have to face them alone. God cares for you just as He cares for my family and me, and He is always faithful! I would like to share with you some of the things I have learned through the years I've walked with the Lord, and I want to encourage you that not only does God have a special purpose for your life, He will show you every step of the way! There is nothing better than knowing that your life is pleasing to the Lord.

While I was in college, my favorite scripture was Jeremiah 33:3—"Call to Me, and I will answer you, and show you great and mighty things, which you do not know." Many years later, I have now experienced the truth of this amazing scripture in my life. Every morning my husband and I sit and talk about the great and mighty things God has done, as well as the many things He continues to teach us. It hasn't all been easy. God has led us to some very difficult and challenging places. But through it all, we have learned how to walk with God and be obedient to Him. And after these many years, we have the privilege of looking back and seeing how everything, both the good and the bad, works together for God's purposes.

As we walk through these pages together, my prayer is that you will see that real-life challenges come to all of us, not only inside the home but outside, and that you will see how God makes the difference in every situation. There are times of laughter and heartache, of struggle and triumph, but through it all, there is a faithful God who loves us. Many of you could also tell numerous stories of how God has worked in your lives, and I hope that this book will encourage you to remain faithful to Him. For those of you who are at the beginning of your spiritual journey, I hope this book will help you desire more of God and not settle for anything less than His best!

—MARILYNN BLACKABY

During a trip to Germany to visit our family, my mother was asked to lead a women's retreat for all the missionaries in the area. She spoke from her heart and out of her experience with the Lord. Her sharing brought encouragement and a time of refreshing, as well as a challenge to remain faithful to the Lord. It was a powerful time that I have not forgotten.

My mother has led countless conferences and has encouraged, counseled, loved, and cried with many people through the years.

She understands the tough times, and she understands how to go through these experiences with the Lord. As well as being a pastor's wife and a partner in the ministry, she has also raised five children to understand the love of the Lord. This is quite a feat, in my opinion!

With the writing of this book come many prayers that it would be an encouragement to all women who are in the middle of God's activity and would like to hear from one who can testify to God's faithfulness. This is not a biography. Our goal is to tell life stories in a way that will reflect the biblical principles that have directed my mother's life. We will also seek to answer many of the questions that have been asked throughout the years:

How did you raise all five children to serve the Lord?

How did you get everything done and not allow your relationship with the Lord to suffer?

How did you know God's will?

How did you remain faithful to the Lord in the midst of crises?

We have also included some examples of women whom God has used through the ages—some from Scripture, and others from different periods of history to the present day. We hope that by seeing examples of faithful women, it will become clear that God chooses ordinary women to accomplish extraordinary things. He can use anyone He chooses to accomplish His purpose; we must only obey Him. We hope that through these stories, you will find laughter and encouragement for your own life and your daily walk with the Lord. So join us now as we sit around the kitchen table with my mom, and she shares her spiritual journey.

—CARRIE BLACKABY WEBB

1

THE PURPOSE
OF LIFE

*To everything there is a season, a time
for every purpose under heaven.*
—*Ecclesiastes 3:1*

"Please don't pray anymore that Marilynn will survive," the doctor told my parents. "If she does recover, the high fever she has will have destroyed her mind."

Just after my fifth birthday, I became extremely ill. At first the doctors weren't overly concerned, because both my brother and sister had the flu, and they assumed I had the same thing. However, when my mother couldn't get me out of the fetal position, and I was unresponsive to her appeals, my parents rushed me to the hospital and found that my appendix had ruptured and my condition was critical.

The hospital was sparsely staffed because of World War II, which compounded the gravity of the situation. The doctors fought to save my life, but no one thought I would survive. A special nurse was assigned to me, and on three separate occasions, she went out to the nurses' station to resign because she couldn't bear the thought of being in the room when I died. It was my godly mother who never left my side, day or night. She constantly prayed for me regardless of what the doctors told her, and she asked for God's will to be done.

After 15 days, I finally awakened from my coma and saw my mother sitting beside me. She looked at me, and her first words were, "Marilynn, God has saved your life for a purpose. You must always do whatever He wants you to do."

"For I know the thoughts that I think toward you,"
says the LORD, "thoughts of peace and not
of evil, to give you a future and a hope."
—*Jeremiah 29:11*

GOD HAD A SPECIAL PURPOSE
FOR MY LIFE

That day I told the Lord that I would do whatever He wanted me to do and that He could have my life and my future. I was only five and didn't know how to read, but from that moment on, I talked to God, and He always answered (Jeremiah 33:3). It set a pattern for my life that continues to this day. For many years, I didn't tell anyone that I talked to God and He talked to me, because *Experiencing God* had not been written yet, and I didn't know that talking to God was okay! I was afraid that people would think there was something wrong with me. Yet from this point on, I truly believed that God had a special plan for my life. Through the years, the doctors' warnings about the high fevers destroying my mind have provided me with a wonderful excuse for my forgetfulness, because I have a doctor's explanation!

I've always been so grateful my mother told me that God had saved my life for a purpose. Those words have come back to me when I have faced difficult decisions, and they have helped me seek God's direction for my life. Before my mother passed away, I was given the opportunity to talk to her about how special this experience was to me. She also remembered how God had impressed on her to share those words and what He had revealed to her during those difficult days by my bedside. Understanding that God had a special purpose for me set the course for my life. I realize that God has a plan for everyone's life, but because of my brush with death, I grew up with the exciting realization that I needed to walk closely with Him so I would know what He wanted me to do.

> *He who heeds the word wisely will find good,*
> *and whoever trusts in the LORD, happy is he.*
> *—Proverbs 16:20*

THE IMPORTANCE OF THE CHURCH

God chose to place me in a family that had a deep love and respect for the Lord (Genesis 17:7; 2 Timothy 1:5). Just as my mother ingrained in me the knowledge that God had a special plan for my life, my father taught me how important it was to grow and mature in my relationship with the Lord through the church. Although our family was not able to afford a car when my sister and I were small, it never stopped my father from doing what he saw as his responsibility. All through my early years, my parents would carry my older sister and me to church every time the doors were open. Fellowshipping and learning from other believers were so important to my parents that they willingly made the sacrifice to get us to church.

A few years later, when my brother was born, my father was finally able to buy a car. I remember him making several trips each

Sunday to different neighborhoods, picking up all the adults and children who didn't have a way to get to church. My father didn't want people saying that they couldn't attend church because they didn't have a ride. He believed that missions was the assignment of

MADAME JEANNE GUYON
(1648–1717)

Madame Guyon[1] was born into French high society and raised in Catholic schools and convents. As a girl, she sought after God and His direction. She so desired to be like Christ, she attached a piece of paper, inscribed with His name, to her shirt as a continual reminder of Him and His will. Through much tribulation and sorrow, she grew to believe that with quiet reflection and time before the Lord, one can obtain spiritual perfection. That is, all can stand blameless before the Lord—not sinless, but blameless. All must seek God Himself and not just His gifts. We must be nothing ourselves before we can receive His fullness. For years Madame Guyon taught that inward holiness regulates our outward life, and that holiness is based on faith alone. She was later imprisoned when church leaders became jealous of her popularity, and her early books were burned. Yet her life and writings profoundly influenced many of God's future leaders, among them John Wesley, Andrew Murray, Hudson Taylor, Watchman Nee, and Adoniram Judson. Although she never asked to be justified before others, God did justify her and allowed her influence to span the generations.[2]

every believer and helping others find the Lord was essential for every Christian.

When we moved from Oklahoma to California, where the churches were smaller than where I grew up, my father told us that if we felt called to be missionaries, we might as well get started. Making friends, bringing them to church, and telling them about Jesus became a way of life for us. If God brought others into our lives, it was our responsibility to share the good news of Christ with them. The simple belief that sharing Christ was our responsibility, combined with seeing at an early age how God worked through our lives, helped prepare me for the path that God had laid out for my life.

"Before I formed you in the womb I knew you."
—Jeremiah 1:5

GOD'S PURPOSE FOR ME IN MARRIAGE

Knowing that God had a plan for my life, I couldn't help but be excited about the future. No matter what it included—an interesting career, a husband and family, or living the missionary life alone on the plains of Africa—I was ready! I had no doubt that whatever God planned, it would be an adventure, and His will for my life would be perfect. I was young and energetic, and although I knew there would be difficult days ahead, I was ready to serve the Lord. I also believed that if God prepared a husband for me, I would know and clearly recognize whom He had provided when the time came. Because of this, I decided not to date seriously or outside of a group setting in the same way many of my friends did but to wait until I knew that God had brought the right person to me. While attending college in California, I knew that I wanted to marry, but I also knew that I would rather stay single than get involved with the wrong man.

During Christmas break, in 1958, my older sister was getting married to a man who attended a seminary in San Francisco. I was so excited for her and thrilled to be involved in her wedding. It just so happened that her fiancé's roommate was to be the best man. Some of my girlfriends had met his roommate, and I asked them if I would like him. They all said, "No, Marilynn, he's much too quiet for you!" But when I met Henry Blackaby, I knew he was not only the best man for my sister's fiancé, but he was the best man for me as well. Two months later, we were engaged, even though we lived five hundred miles apart.

God made it clear to me—not only in my heart and through what He was saying to me in prayer, but also through what I read in Scripture—that Henry was the man He had for me. And it was clear not only to me and to Henry but to everyone around us as well.

Marrying Henry was the easiest decision I had ever made, and the most important one, next to my decision to follow Christ. For not only was God providing me with a husband, He was also presenting me with a ministry partner and a godly father for our future children. There were purposes that God could accomplish only through us as a couple. He knew there would be difficult times that would require a strong marriage to survive. He also knew that we would have five children who would need the foundation of a strong Christian home for all He would call them to do as He worked out His purposes in their lives.

Then he said, "The God of our fathers has chosen
you that you should know His will, and see the Just
One, and hear the voice of His mouth."
—*Acts 22:14*

GOD'S LONG-TERM PREPARATION

God prepares our lives, bringing us through experiences for reasons that we don't completely comprehend. Looking back, the path God took Henry and me down is easy to recognize, but at the time, all we knew to do was to be obedient and trust Him to lead us.

The year my sister was married, I applied for a summer missions program through my college. I believed that God wanted me to be involved in missions, but I didn't know where. I decided not to select a location on my application but to leave the place of service up to the Lord. I faced a complication, however, because the missions interview was scheduled to take place during the wedding celebrations. I had to make a decision, but I knew I could never miss something so important to my family as my sister's wedding.

Although I was disappointed not to be able to go to the interview, I knew that God would show me what He wanted me to do. What I didn't know was that because the people in charge of the missions program knew me, they bypassed the interview process and assigned me to a place they had never sent anyone before. Much to my amazement, they sent me to the northwest section of Washington State, but technically my position of service was over the Canadian border in the city of Vancouver. I was thrilled to go to Canada, and through this experience, God gave me an amazing opportunity to see what our denomination's pioneer work there was like.

That summer I took so many surveys that I wore out a pair of shoes! I also worked with three two-week Vacation Bible Schools for children in different locations. The work was difficult, and I saw through this experience that Canada truly is a different country. The work, the attitudes, the churches, the culture, the responses, and the spiritual traditions—everything was completely different from my experience in the United States. God had a special purpose for my life that summer, and it will always stand out in my mind.

Although Henry was still attending seminary in California, I was able to arrange to meet his family in Vancouver for the first time. Henry's family is Canadian, so they were quite interested in getting acquainted with the American girl who had captured Henry's heart. I was also able to meet and work alongside the church leadership of my denomination in Canada. Little did I know at the time that I was about to join them in ministry there and would be working with them for several years to come. Quite a few years later, my oldest son's doctoral dissertation traced the history of our denomination in Canada. Much to my amazement, as I read his work, I realized that I knew all of the names he mentioned, and I remembered the work in those early developmental years. What a privilege to be part of it!

This experience also provided me with years of laughter. Among the small group of missionaries who were sent to work in Canada that summer was a young man who was assigned to Saskatoon, Saskatchewan. We mercilessly teased him, insisting that he would drop off the end of the world way out there, and we would never see him again! We never did see or hear from him again, which just confirmed our suspicions. Ironically, 12 years later, people told Henry and me the same thing as God led us to work in Saskatoon!

> *[God] chose us in [Christ] before the foundation*
> *of the world, that we should be holy and*
> *without blame before Him in love.*
> *—Ephesians 1:4*

> *[God] made known to us the mystery of His will,*
> *according to His good pleasure which*
> *He purposed in Himself.*
> *—Ephesians 1:9*

SEEING GOD'S ACTIVITY

After a few years in Saskatoon, our home was continually filled with kids. Not only did we have five children of our own, but I often cared for the two boys across the street and any of my children's other friends who wanted to come over. Our older three boys shared bedrooms in the basement, which also contained a small game and recreation area. With both our front and side doors located off the kitchen, where I was usually working, I often felt like the gatekeeper for all who wanted to spend time at our house.

One day, instead of opening the door and sending a friend of my boys straight downstairs, I stopped and asked him how he was doing. Almost immediately he began to share something he was struggling with. Although I was incredibly busy, God nudged me to stop what I was doing and take some time to listen to this hurting and troubled youth. We sat together at the kitchen table, and I put everything on hold while we talked. Two hours later, when the boys came up for dinner, they were surprised to find their friend, whom they assumed had never arrived.

Dinner that evening was late and quickly thrown together, but I was glad I didn't allow my responsibilities to distract me from God's activity. Clearly, only God working in this teenage boy's life could have caused him to share with me all that he needed to that day. After that experience, I always took time to ask guests how they were doing, and every now and then my boys would find their friends sharing with me around our kitchen table.

> *God's intent for every Christian is straightforward: He wants us to have a real and personal relationship with Him.*

To know that God has a plan for our lives and to understand that purpose is the heartfelt desire of most Christians. We want to obey God's call and purpose for us, if only we knew what it was. God's intent for every Christian is straightforward: He wants us to have a real and personal relationship with Him (Colossians 1:24–27; Romans 1:6). It's that simple. When we have a deep and growing relationship with the Lord, He will guide us throughout each day.

When we faithfully obey Him, He will reveal more and more of His nature and His ways to us. As we mature, so does the way He works in our lives, and this leads to an exciting life with Christ.

As busy as I was as a pastor's wife and mother of five, I could easily have come to resent the fact that so many other children kept showing up on my doorstep. Instead, God opened my eyes to the significant work He was doing in the lives of these young people, and He invited me to join Him in that activity.

God wants us to understand His plan—even in the little things. Before He gave me the wisdom and insight to help the boy I mentioned earlier, He waited for me to obey—to stop my own activity and listen. Often, it's difficult to realize that God waits for us to obey, and possibly repent of something in our lives, before He will use us for His purpose.

We can easily miss God's activity if we're not actively aware and looking for it. Sometimes we can miss God's activity because we tend to make things more complicated than they actually are (Philippians 3:8–10, Luke 10:38–42). We can be so concerned about finding God's will for our lives that we don't pay attention to what God has placed right in front of us. Being preoccupied with daily responsibilities can leave us unaware

Trusting in our abilities can often keep us from depending on the Lord for His strength and guidance.

of what God is doing around us (Philippians 3:8–10). We can also be so involved with church programs and weekly activities that we miss what God wants us to do. We can be so focused on what *we* think we're gifted at doing that we fail to recognize when God is seeking to do a fresh work through our lives by using our weaknesses. God only equips us for His assignments as we obey Him, not before. Trusting in our abilities can often keep us from depending on the Lord for His strength and guidance (Psalm 25:9).

The example of Moses, who turned aside from his work to encounter God and to receive God's invitation, still applies to us today. When Moses saw the burning bush, he turned aside to see this great sight (Exodus 3:1–4). God talked to Moses only after he stopped what he had been doing and came to Him. In this same way, God will also extend to us an invitation to join Him and His activity. We must adjust our lives, no matter what we're involved with at the time, and follow Him.

> *So when the LORD saw that he [Moses] turned aside to look, God called to him from the midst of the bush and said, "Moses, Moses!" And he said, "Here I am."*
> —*Exodus 3:4*

WHAT IS GOD'S PURPOSE?

As I've talked with many people around the world, the questions I'm most often asked are: "How did you know God's purpose for your life?" and "How can I know what God wants me to do?" Simply put, it's a daily process that God will reveal as you grow in your love relationship through obedience.

While I was visiting our daughter in Germany several years ago, I was filled with the sense that God wanted me to be part of a missions trip. I discussed it with her, commenting that this was the first time God had asked me to be involved in a missions venture without my husband. I had no idea what it would entail, but I knew God was preparing me for something, and I was ready to obey. I flew home, and the next day I received a call from a leader in my church. He needed me to go on a missions trip to Cambodia to teach smocking and sewing. If I hadn't been prepared by the Lord for this call, I wouldn't have been ready for this development. Instead, I knew that the Lord wanted me to go on this trip, and after sharing with my husband, I signed up to go.

I encountered many roadblocks in the months between the decision to go and the actual trip. In fact, if I had relied on logic, I would have canceled. First of all, there were some serious health complications with several members of the team, and my husband had also been seriously ill in the hospital. In addition, after the tickets were booked, I was told of an oversight that had occurred in my schedule. I was due to return to Atlanta two hours *after* I was to leave for a two-week trip to Africa. I had to change my tickets to come home one day early, without the rest of the team. This left me with only 22 hours to wash clothes and prepare for the other trip. But in spite of these difficulties, I knew that God wanted me to go on this trip.

I worked harder than I've ever worked on any project. It took months to get together the materials and the equipment needed to teach the class. Never having taught something like this before, I spent countless hours preparing my presentations and considering how to best demonstrate the new techniques. It was an exciting challenge for me.

While in Cambodia, the rest of the church group worked as a medical team, and I was sent to another location to train the local women in smocking and sewing, skills that would help them earn a living. This was the first time I had done anything like this—especially without my husband. I worked from 8:00 A.M. to 5:00 P.M. every day in the heat and communicated through a translator. Yet I know that God blessed my time there. The women were deeply appreciative, and it gave me an open door to share the love of Christ. Since this trip, the women have used their ability to sell clothing and other handmade things at the local craft fairs, and the smocking and sewing have brought more money into the community than the locals would make in months of work. It gave the believers working in the area an open door to establish relationships as well as help the community have a better way of life. Through this experience, God allowed me to be part of something I had always dreamed of doing: serving on the international mission field with indigenous people.

God loves me, and it was out of His love for me that He sent me to represent Him and share His love through practical means. Scripture tells us that out of our love relationship with God, He will reveal His ways and His purpose for our lives. We can see many examples of this relationship in Scripture: Abraham, through whom He created a nation for Himself; Moses, who was used of God to lead His people out of captivity; Esther, who was chosen by God to save His people from annihilation; Mary, through whom God sent His Son into the world; the apostle Paul, who ultimately wrote much of the New Testament and was chosen to take the gospel message to the world; and countless other examples. That should be a huge weight off our shoulders! We don't have to be stressed out trying to find God's will for our lives. What we need to be seeking is God Himself. If we're pursuing the Lord and His righteousness, then everything will be added to us (Matthew 6:33)—including knowing His will for our lives.

God speaks to us in many different ways (Hebrews 1:1–2), and when He does, we ought to embrace what He has for us. God's ways are always best! At times, He knows we don't have the faith and trust to follow where He is leading, so He will wait to reveal something new to us. If we truly want to follow the Lord, we don't get to pick and choose the way we go; we can only follow Him (Matthew 4:18–22). That's what being obedient is all about.

> *Then his brothers also went and fell down before his*
> *face, and they said, "Behold, we are your servants."*
> *Joseph said to them, "Do not be afraid, for am I in the*
> *place of God? But as for you, you meant evil against*
> *me; but God meant it for good, in order to bring it*
> *about as it is this day, to save many people alive."*
> *— Genesis 50:18–20*

GOD HAS A PURPOSE FOR US TODAY

As you read through these pages, you may be able to completely relate to some of the things I've talked about. You may have grown up in a Christian home where one or both parents helped nurture in you the same sense of purpose I had. But if that was not your reality, God can still use your life for Him, even without the influence of a Christian upbringing. What is most important to God isn't *when* you chose to trust Him but that you love Him *now* with all of your heart.

God's ways haven't changed, nor have His purposes. The same God who purposed to build a nation from Abraham is the same God who intended that I would survive my trauma at age five. The same God who revealed Himself to Jeanne Guyon, who influenced countless people to seek holiness in their lives, is the same God who encounters our lives today. We can always count on God to have a plan and to complete it, and His plan will often be completely different from what we're expecting.

God has a purpose for our lives, and He wants us to know what His will is (Ephesians 2:10). He won't hide it from us and leave us confused and uncertain, but we must watch for His activity and obey Him. Our job is not to seek God's will but rather to seek after God Himself (Matthew 6:33). We must live before the Lord in such a way that when He reveals His plan to us, we have nothing in our lives that would hinder our obedience to him. God isn't concerned with our "doing" His will; He is concerned with who we are in Christ. When our hearts are completely centered in God, He will use us to complete His purposes, which will always lead to a deeper and more meaningful relationship with Him. God's purpose is for something much greater than we could imagine, and we could never accomplish it without taking the steps to grow in our relationship with Him. Spiritual maturity doesn't happen overnight; it happens with each little step of obedience, and we're all on this journey together!

> *The LORD of hosts has sworn,*
> *saying, "Surely, as I have thought,*
> *so it shall come to pass, and as I*
> *have purposed, so it shall stand."*
> —*Isaiah 14:24*

QUESTIONS FOR DEEPER REFLECTION

1. Knowing that God is more concerned with your character than with what you can do for Him, how have you recognized or experienced God shaping who you are? In what ways has He accomplished this? What characteristics is He currently working on?

2. God works daily in and around our lives. Often, the little things make the biggest impact on lives around us: taking time to listen to another person, asking the right questions, turning aside in the middle of a busy day to refocus our attention on the Lord. As you evaluate your day, are you careful with the "little things"? Did God bring an opportunity your way today that allowed Him to work through you to touch another person? If not, ask Him to give you a chance to make an impact on others every day, and commit to obey Him when the opportunities come your way.

Questions for Group Discussion

1. Since God has an eternal purpose for each of us, it should cause us to live with the expectation of seeing Him work through our lives. How do you see God working out His purposes in your lives?

2. Discuss how a challenging situation you are currently facing is causing you to trust the Lord more and grow in your Christian walk and relationship with Christ.

3. No matter what our background is, God has a plan to bring each of us joy and completeness in Him. If God has helped you overcome something from your past, please share how He has healed you and made you stronger.

2

THE KEY TO SUCCESS

"He who has My commandments and keeps them, it is he who loves Me. And he who loves Me will be loved by My Father, and I will love him and manifest Myself to him."
— John 14:21

At the time God called Henry and me into missions, we were pastoring our second church in Southern California. That year, we attended a foreign-missions emphasis week at our denomination's conference center in Glorietta, New Mexico. It was a fun time that gave us a chance to see friends and hear what God was doing in other parts of the world. The keynote speaker that week, Dr. Cauthen, said something that really made an impression on our hearts: "God has already told you to go in the Great Commission, so if you are staying here, you'd better have His permission." As Henry and I prayed together, we realized we no longer felt we had God's permission to stay in California.

We had been involved in ministry together for 10 years, and God was blessing the church and adding weekly to our numbers. It was exciting and fulfilling to see God at work, both in our lives and in the lives of the church members. But our missions call was strong, and since I had studied and sought to be involved in missions all my life, I was excited to respond to God's invitation.

We immediately contacted our denomination's international missions board and started the application process for international work. Then we faced a crisis: Our oldest son became ill just as we completed the application hurdles and had a position reserved for us in Africa. It was a huge crisis for us; no one could determine the cause of his condition or what we should do about it. Because of this, the missions board put our application on hold until we could pass the medical clearance. Knowing that God had called us to be involved in missions, we waited until He told us what our next step should be.

Two months after our application was put on hold, we received a call from a friend who was concerned about the Christian work in Canada. Canadians who had been called to the ministry were often going to the States for their training, and many were not returning to their homeland. Few people were willing to work in the more difficult locations in Canada, and there were so few leaders left to lead the churches in our denomination that several churches had been without a pastor for years.

Our friend mentioned a church in Saskatoon that was down to 10 members, and he asked if we would allow the congregation to consider Henry as their pastor. This small congregation was so discouraged that they had decided to meet together and pray about disbanding the church and selling the building. But after they got up off their knees, they unanimously decided that if Henry would come as pastor, they would try one more time. This wasn't an easy decision for them because the two pastors they had called during the previous five years didn't stay and had left a hurting church behind them.

Henry was invited to meet with the congregation in January of 1970. (The day of the meeting, the temperature was 40 below zero!) The meeting confirmed in Henry's heart that Saskatoon was where God wanted us, and after praying together, we decided to accept the position.

When the decision became public, we were surprised that some people were against our following God's call to Canada! Two men who really loved Henry and appreciated his work drove five hundred miles to talk some sense into him. They truly believed that Henry shouldn't leave a good church and a position where he was respected, only to be lost in the wilds of Canada. Ironically, their remarks were surprisingly similar to what I had told another young missionary 12 years earlier! They said, "You'll get lost, and no one will ever hear from you again. You'll never get a chance to come back to the States." Henry's response was, "Well, God will know where we are."

The move was anything but easy. I was highly emotional during the drive to Saskatoon. I cried for the first 250 miles, probably causing Henry to question his sanity! I was beginning to question my own state of mind because although I would miss our family and friends, I was looking forward to following the Lord on this adventure. I didn't realize at the time that I was pregnant with our fifth child!

The tiny church in Saskatoon couldn't afford to help with moving expenses or pay us much of a salary for the first year. In fact, the month before we came, the total offerings for the month were ninety dollars. Making things even more difficult, we found out after we arrived that a couple of people in the church hadn't believed we would accept the call and unhappily left when the other members wouldn't sell the building. They did eventually return when they saw God working in the church, but the situation was challenging, and the people were tired of getting their hopes up. Although they did call Henry as pastor, their previous disappointment was hard to overcome. The one thing that helped us endure that first difficult year was knowing we were where God wanted us to be.

"Obey My voice, and do according to all that I command you; so shall you be My people, and I will be your God."
—Jeremiah 11:4

UNDERSTANDING OBEDIENCE FROM GOD'S PERSPECTIVE

Obedience. This word seems to have many different meanings depending on one's culture or experience. For some, the word *obedience* can have negative connotations. It can bring back memories of an extremely difficult or abusive childhood. For others, the word may bring to mind a picture of a military chain of command and obedience without question—or it may conjure images of receiving the punishment for disobedience. In a society that prides itself on freedom, the concept of obedience can sound demeaning. Obedience can often be linked with discipline, especially when we are teaching our children to obey. We often interpret the meaning of obedience, positively or negatively, through our own perspective and experiences.

When we look at Scripture and God's words to us, we need to view things from God's viewpoint. How is He different from all the others who have tried to control us throughout our lives? Why does He tell us to do the things He does? Why should we obey His voice? Because only God has the wisdom and knowledge to guide us in perfect love. Others may love us and want what's best for us, but only the Lord is all-knowing and sees the future. He wants to give us His best, and only He knows the path that leads us into His perfect will (Deuteronomy 5:32–33). The only way we can obtain

His best is if we follow Him and His voice. If we do not obey Him, we can't receive what He wants to give us. God isn't a belligerent or abusive father, or a strict officer enforcing His commands, or

MARY, MOTHER OF JESUS

*Behold the maidservant of the Lord! Let it be
to me according to your word. (Luke 1:38)*

Mary was a young teen when she heard what God was about to do in her life. She could have had many responses to the revelation that she was about to become pregnant before she was wed and would give birth to the Son of God. Yet she accepted the word from the Lord as truth and obeyed Him.

Mary lived a life of obedience. Although she would have faced ridicule and been ostracized from her family and friends because of her pregnancy, she remained steadfast in the Lord. God knew Mary's heart, and He knew that He could trust her with the most important task: raising Jesus, His Son.

When we see Mary mentioned in the Gospels, she is striving to raise Jesus according to the Scriptures, and she is being obedient to the Jewish laws. When something new was revealed to her, she kept it in her heart. When she went through the experience of seeing her son killed, she didn't turn away from God. Instead, she obeyed the Lord and became part of the early church.

Although she may not have understood the whys of what God was doing around her, she trusted and obeyed through the difficulties, and God honored her obedience and faithfulness.[1]

someone trying to control us for His benefit. God acts out of perfect love to protect and provide His best for us. He wants to bless us and see us succeed at what He knows will bring us complete fulfillment. Obedience to God brings life—even if His directions don't always seem to make sense to us at the time.

> *Has the LORD as great delight in burnt offerings*
> *and sacrifices, as in obeying the voice of*
> *the LORD? Behold, to obey is better than sacrifice,*
> *and to heed than the fat of rams.*
> —*1 Samuel 15:22*

GROWING SPIRITUALLY REQUIRES OBEDIENCE, NOT HUMAN REASONING

Our move to Canada defied logic. If we had trusted in logic and people's opinions about our move, we would have never left a church that was full of people who loved us. Yet we knew what God wanted us to do, and even the two people who later decided they didn't want Henry to come as pastor couldn't stand in the way of God's plan and our obedience to it!

To grow in our relationship with the Lord, we must obey Him. If Henry and I had made a list of pros and cons regarding our move to Canada, we could easily have listed one hundred different cons but only one pro: God told us to go.

This move was seen by some as a huge step down for Henry's career. Not only did we leave a secure position of influence in our denomination to be "forgotten in the wilds of Canada," but we also left a large and healthy church to pastor a tiny, discouraged congregation. In fact, our family alone almost doubled the attendance. The move also took us away from family and friends and the warm weather of Southern California and plunged us into the bitterly cold winters of Saskatoon. And to make things more difficult, we had no secure finances to support a family of seven. There truly was no logic to this move.

Yet now we look back on that time in our lives and see that this was how God planned to bless us and allow us to grow in our Christian faith. The lessons and experiences from the 12 years we spent in that church in Saskatoon were foundational for the book *Experiencing God* that Henry would write 20 years later. And it led us to our current work in helping people understand God's call on their lives.

Although we saw daily blessings during the early years of our work in Saskatoon, it took several years before God began doing a major work through our church. It was often an extremely challenging, exhausting, and sometimes painful time in our lives. (I'll go into much greater detail in the following chapter about this crucial time of learning in our lives.) But it was worth the sacrifice. God honored our obedience beyond all we could think or imagine (John 12:26) by continuing to use us for His work. We wouldn't have had the opportunities we have today—speaking at the United Nations, meeting world leaders, writing, and sharing God's love with people around the world—if we hadn't been obedient to what God told us to do back then. He knew what His long-term plans for our lives were, and we needed to be in Canada to experience His will.

GOD'S PLAN INVOLVES OTHERS

Robert and Corene Cannon, a young couple who were serving as student directors at a large university in Texas, heard my husband speak at a conference and decided to come to Saskatoon to help us for six weeks in the summer of 1975. During those weeks, God moved so strongly in their hearts that they decided to leave their established jobs in Texas to come work with us. Even though they had no guarantee of a salary, they chose to sell their house and obey God's leading in their lives. God blessed their obedience! He provided them with a house at a very good price, and He met their financial needs in amazing ways. Over the next five years, God blessed their student ministry by leading almost two hundred students to accept the Lord and calling around one hundred into full-time Christian service. Today we meet many of those former students all over the world as they serve the Lord in different ways.

God used Robert and Corene not only to bless our church and the lives of the students but also to encourage us and share the ministry work. We found out years later that another couple had felt God's call to come work with us before the Cannons, but for whatever reason, they chose not to answer the call. God used this couple in other ways, but there is no way to know what He would have done if they had answered the call to join what He was about to do in Saskatoon.

Keep your heart with all diligence,
for out of it spring the issues of life.
— Proverbs 4:23

MARY SLESSOR
(1848–1915)

Mary was a Scottish Presbyterian mill worker, born into poverty and misery.[2] Although her mother instilled in Mary a love for God and mission work, her father was a drunk and terrorized her early years. In spite of this, she grew into a gentle, sensitive, and loving person with a deep empathy for children and the oppressed.[3] God called Mary into missions work, and at the age of 28, she went alone to serve in the unreached region of Calabar (now Nigeria).

As she began her difficult work to be a lighthouse in a dark land, results came only through toil, patience, and prayer. "Christ was never in a hurry," she wrote.[4] Calabar was filled with witchcraft, secret societies, drunkenness, and filth, yet Mary was filled with love for the people. Because the people believed that twins were evil and should be killed at birth, she adopted and raised them as her own to show that they, too, were God's children.

Although she never had much money, she said, "What is money to God? The difficult thing is to make men and women."[5] She started churches and schools, helped bring law and order in the country, raised the status of African women, and educated many in the Christian life. Her ministry ran from "preaching to patching."[6] Through her love, wisdom, and prayers, she won over the cruelest people of the bush country. She became known as "White Ma of Calabar," and her influence and ministry stretched for two thousand miles in West Africa.[7]

OUR CHARACTER DEPENDS ON
OUR OBEDIENCE

God had many plans for our lives that He was preparing us for. Because our move was so illogical and the work we were doing so different, we were always asked to explain how we knew that God was speaking to us, how we knew God's will. God knew that we needed to experience more of Him to be able to help others understand as well. We learned that before you can share a biblical truth with others, you must live it out daily in your own life (1 John 2:3–6).

As I mentioned earlier, while we were still living in California, one of our sons became ill. After he had his tonsils removed he experienced secondary problems that concerned the doctors. Although they were unsure of the root cause of his symptoms, they put him on heavy medication that brought on serious side effects. Because of this, our missions application for Africa had to be put on hold, and God later used this situation to turn our attention on Saskatoon.

When we arrived in Canada, we took our son to a doctor to see if a Canadian medical expert could help him with his mysterious condition. After running several tests, we were told that there was nothing wrong with him, and there never had been. At that point, we could have called our missions board and requested permission to pursue our previous appointment in Africa—with a full salary and insurance! But we knew God had used that experience in our lives to get us to where He wanted us to be.

Over the years, many people have shared with me their struggles to obey something the Lord has revealed to them. They describe wrestling with God over what He has said, being unsettled for days, struggling to find out why God would ask a certain thing of them. If we are uncertain about what God is saying, waiting on Him for understanding is crucial. However, when God's direction is clear, we need to trust and follow Him. Struggling to obey God's leading is a direct reflection of our trust relationship with Him. God knows our situation, and He is aware of our responsibilities. He also understands all the excuses we give—but He doesn't accept our disobedience.

When God speaks to us, His timing is perfect (Galatians 4:4). The time for us to obey is when He reveals His will. When God asks us to share our faith with someone, we shouldn't wait until we feel comfortable or more prepared before we obey. We don't know what God is doing in the heart of that individual at that moment. When God asks us to attend or lead a Bible study, we shouldn't wait until we feel ready; we should just obey. When we feel that God is leading us, we don't need to explain to the Lord about our job or other time commitments or our busy family situation. If we wrestle with God or our obedience to His call, the time may pass and the opportunity to serve in the same way may never arise again.

MISSING THE CHANCE

Regrettably, it's all too easy to find excuses for why we can't obey the Lord when we don't think through our decisions and how they may affect the future. But God has a reason for even the smallest of His commands. I remember a time when He gently asked me to talk with a gentleman about his marriage and the responsibilities that came with that commitment. I knew I was one of the few people this man would listen to, although others had tried unsuccessfully to help. But at the time, I was tired and had been helping his wife deal with a stressful situation. This couple lived almost two hours from me, and when I was needed, I had to find someone to watch my children. It wasn't easy. And to complicate matters, I wasn't too pleased with this man and didn't want to talk to him!

I put off obeying, and time passed. When we moved to another city, it was too late to talk to him, and I missed my window of opportunity. I can tell you that even 20 years later, I still grieve over not obeying that clear urging from the Lord. Just because He spoke quietly to me about it did not mean that the situation was unimportant. The things that are little in our eyes are just as important to the Lord as the bigger things. All these years later, I still wonder if God could have used me to make a difference in that marriage, and if I could have helped in some way to save my friends from years of heartache. After learning this lesson, I have always tried to obey even the smallest whisper from the Lord.

> *And [these blessings] shall come to pass if you*
> *diligently obey the voice of the LORD your God.*
> *—Zechariah 6:15*

DOES GOD CALL ONE SPOUSE AND NOT THE OTHER?

Probably the biggest struggle that married women tell me about is that their spouses aren't walking with the Lord, and they don't see how God can use their lives under those conditions. Maybe at one time they felt a call to missions or to some kind of Christian service, but because of their present situations, they don't know how to follow through with the earlier call. Can God, or will God, still use their lives for His purposes?

The important thing to remember is that God is more concerned with our being than our doing. A good biblical example is the life of Joseph. Joseph had a dream that he would rule over his brothers one day, yet because of their jealousy and hatred for him, he was sold into slavery, falsely accused, and confined in prison. He spent 12 years of his life as a convict. Yet he never rejected God or His will and still sought to live a life pleasing to Him. Joseph wasn't in a position to "do" much for God, yet God was working on his character. Eventually, God fulfilled the vision He gave to Joseph, but the process didn't look like anything Joseph could have imagined (see Genesis 37–47).

> *The important thing to remember is that God is more concerned with our being than our doing.*

God takes us from where we are and builds our character so He can involve us in His mighty work. If you became a Christian after you were married and want to know if God will use your life for His kingdom purposes, the answer is *yes*! Practice daily obedience to all that God reveals to you. If you are regularly seeking to please the Lord, God will use your life to bless others. God will always bless and work through those who are seeking after Him.

If you became a Christian early in life, yet you strayed from God and became unequally yoked in marriage, God can and will

God takes us from where we are and builds our character so He can involve us in His mighty work.

still use your life to accomplish His purposes if you obey Him. If you felt called as a child to some form of Christian service, your calling will change to match your present situation. Your marriage is important to the Lord, as are your

marriage vows. If one spouse is more in tune with the Lord than the other, even though both are Christians, God will give you an assignment that you can complete as a married person. God will not divide your marriage.

If you feel the call to be involved in missions, look around you. No matter where you live, there are people who need to know the Lord. Sometimes the biggest mission field is right around the corner! A ministry that is often overlooked is prayer ministry. Why? Because prayer ministry involves the practice of "being" more than of "doing," and tangible results are often difficult to see. We must look past being busy for the Lord and look at being who He wants us to be. When that is firmly in place, we'll be able to see and experience more of God than we could ever have imagined.

"To him the doorkeeper opens, and the sheep
hear his voice; and he calls his own sheep by
name and leads them out. And when he brings

out his own sheep, he goes before them; and the
sheep follow him, for they know his voice."
—John 10:3–4

OBEDIENCE IN SPITE OF DIFFICULTIES

One of the things that God used to help shape us into the couple He wanted us to be was our first church in San Pablo, California. Before we married and while Henry was still in seminary, he had been on staff at the church. He began by teaching a teenage-boys' class, moved into the music- and educational-pastor positions, and then was asked to be the associate pastor. By the time we married, he had been voted in as the pastor. I was only 21 and had just graduated from university 10 days before we were married. I used to tease Henry that he worked his way up the church ladder, always being faithful in what he did and being given new jobs as other leaders left the church. Henry made 10 dollars a week until he was voted in as pastor, and then he made 80 dollars a week. We began serving together in ministry immediately after our honeymoon. I thought life was wonderful, and I was thrilled to be a pastor's wife. It was something that I had always known God had planned for my life. Little did I know how difficult those first years of ministry were going to be.

The former pastor and his wife were still members of the church, deeply involved in its activities, and quite willing to tell us how things should be done. For the next five years, I found that in spite of all my enthusiasm, I still had a great deal to learn. In addition to what God wanted to teach me, I apparently needed help in knowing how to dress, how to greet people at the door, how to sit properly in church, and especially how to raise my children. We had three children while we were at this church, and it was even explained to me that I was having too many!

For quite some time, I felt inadequate and insecure, and I didn't know where I fit in. Yet God had so many things to teach me through these circumstances. Most of our people truly loved us and wanted to see us succeed. God gave us some godly men in the church to help us grow. When we came up with a great idea for how to reach others for the Lord, one of these men would take Henry aside and say, "Yes, we could do that, but have you thought about this?" Without fail, their godly wisdom was better than our ideas. What was truly inspiring was that some of them only had an eighth-grade education, yet God gave them great wisdom in His ways and an amazing understanding of His will. This truth helped us understand that God can use anyone for His purposes, regardless of their background, and that we shouldn't trust in our knowledge, but only in our relationship with the Lord. God used this time for a great purpose in our lives. We needed to know how to listen to and look for what He was doing and not what we thought we could do. Our plans for the church didn't have to be based on the latest fad, but rather, on knowing what God's plan was and obeying it.

I desired to understand my place in God's kingdom. I wasn't just the pastor's wife; I was also God's child. Yes, as the pastor's wife, I had a responsibility to those in the church. But as a child of God, I had the task of serving Him in the way He asked me to. Many people had great plans for how I could effectively serve the church by teaching a women's Bible study or playing the organ or singing in the choir, but God had a different plan. I quickly found out that the only person I had to please was the Lord. He used this time in my life to reveal a new type of ministry for the church: a preschool and children's ministry. Since I had three children at the time, it was important to me that the church have a ministry that would teach simple but essential truths to the children. As I got the ministry organized and well structured, it grew fast, attracting many young families from the community, who were pleased we were a family-oriented church.

Although the early years at our first church were challenging both emotionally and spiritually, God was laying this experience as the foundation for what was to come. Henry and I needed to learn and grow—both as a couple and as church leaders—and this type of learning comes only through experience. What I learned about listening to God's plan rather than other people's opinions of what I should do helped me in future churches. I determined not to jump in where people said I was needed but to wait on the Lord's guidance. My experience structuring the preschool and children's ministry was something that would help me in every church we would serve in.

Knowing that God had a plan and that we didn't have to dream one up for Him deeply impacted us. We stayed at this church for five years, until the Lord led us to a congregation in Southern California. Although we had many challenges ahead of us, God had already placed in us the seeds for building His kingdom. The Lord had built our character through what we experienced, and He had built the deep trust that comes from an intimate love relationship with Him. I'm not sure that we could have been as successful in Canada had God not already carefully laid this foundation of trust in our lives. His purpose wasn't to protect us from challenging situations but to use those situations to mold us into the persons He wanted us to be for His kingdom work.

> *You shall therefore keep His statutes and*
> *His commandments which I command you*
> *today, that it may go well with you and with*
> *your children after you, and that you may prolong*
> *your days in the land which the LORD your*
> *God is giving you for all time.*
> *—Deuteronomy 4:40*

OUR OBEDIENCE RESTS WITH US

In the wonderful ways of God, He allows us to choose whether we want a relationship with Him. If we choose to be in that relationship, we must trust Him and His guidance for our lives. Always think of obedience from God's perspective. Our obedience to Him leads us to abundant life, for God's leading is based on His love for us. His directions are always best and are intended to bring us the greatest blessings (Genesis 12:1–3). Can they be difficult? Yes! His ways may not appear logical to us, and that often distinguishes His ways from ours.

We should obey the moment God asks us to follow Him (Matthew 4:18–22). When we struggle to obey, we can easily miss an incredible experience with the Lord. Immediate obedience reveals our unwavering trust in God, that in His wisdom and love for us, He will only give us His best. Any assignment from God is a tremendous privilege. Obedience to God's commands always leads to a full and meaningful life. If we walk daily in obedience, doing all we know God wants us to do, He will use our lives to complete His purposes.

And being found in appearance as a man,
He humbled Himself and became obedient to the
point of death, even the death of the cross.
—Philippians 2:8

QUESTIONS FOR DEEPER REFLECTION

1. When God encounters us, His timing is always perfect. Looking through your life, can you think of a moment when the timing of your obedience was crucial? Has there been a time when the opportunity to be obedient passed you by and didn't come again? What difference did it make in your life and what have you learned from that experience?

2. If you're married, describe how God is shaping your character and making a positive difference in your life through your marriage. If you're single, describe how God has placed people in your life who can encourage you and keep you walking steadily on His path.

Questions for Group Discussion

1. When you have faced important decisions in the past, in what ways did you allow others to distract or negatively influence you against following what you knew God wanted you to do? Discuss how making a decision based on your own logic, a pros-and-cons list, or input from others has backfired in each of your lives.

2. God honors obedience, even if it comes much later in life. Take a few moments to examine your walk with the Lord and look for moments of blessing. How were some of those blessings a direct result of your obedience?

3

WALKING ONE
DAY AT A TIME

*Then He said to them all, "If anyone
desires to come after Me, let him deny
himself, and take up his cross daily,
and follow Me. For whoever desires to
save his life will lose it, but whoever
loses his life for My sake will save it."*

—Luke 9:23–24

"Help, help!" I heard the frantic cry of one of my children and immediately began searching for the source. Still hearing the cries, I ran outside to the backyard—and there he was. All I could see of him were his blue eyes and white-blond hair as he was sinking neck deep in the mud of our Saskatoon garden. The spring thaw was on, and this wonderful event is known as "breakup." All that meant to me was mud, mud, and more mud. What I didn't understand at the time was that the ground thawed in layers, and with the bottom layer still frozen, there was no place for the water to go. So it created a huge pile of goo that delighted my four boys, who wanted to see how far they could wade until the water and mud covered the top of their boots. They all discovered the limits of their boots, and after our garden dried out, we would go on a rubber-boot hunt to round up the ones that had stuck and sunk in the mud.

The spring thaw and other new experiences like it only emphasized that, although we had been through many different types of situations, Saskatoon was completely different. Henry had completed two seminary degrees, and we had served together in ministry for 10 years when we were called to serve in Saskatoon. But in spite of our years in ministry, it was a testing ground for me because it was quite unlike any other place I had lived.

We had four little boys under the age of eight, and our fifth child was on the way. We arrived in Canada during the late winter in our Southern California clothes. Since, as mentioned in a previous chapter, the church didn't have money for moving expenses or even for a salary, we had to spend the last of our reserves on warm clothes for the children. Fortunately, a state convention agreed to send us around five hundred dollars a month, since our tiny congregation in Saskatoon couldn't afford to pay us that first year. We were thankful that the church owned a parsonage, regardless of the fact that it was an interesting study of colors. The floors were orange, our couch was yellow and orange, and the walls were pink. This was, after all, the 1970s! There were no curtains or blinds when we moved in, and we had only one small bathroom for a family of six—soon to be seven—and our frequent, and often unexpected, guests! Although we were able to finish the basement later on, we experienced a new type of togetherness with only three bedrooms for seven people.

The small church building was also attention grabbing. Originally a dreary white, it had been painted lime green and nicknamed the "green box." The property had had a For Sale sign up for months before we came. In fact, people in the neighborhood thought we had bought the church and were starting something new.

The building certainly had its quirks. During the spring thaw, a few of us would arrive early Sunday morning to mop up the water in the basement, where Sunday school took place. Sunday school would last until the water crept back across the floor to our feet. When we were surrounded by water, it was our cue to dismiss class and flee the basement for the upstairs auditorium to begin the morning worship service. It was impossible to adequately heat the building in the winter and impossible to keep it cool during the summer. But God was always present and helped us deal with one situation at a time.

ELIZABETH

And they [Zacharias and Elizabeth] were both righteous
before God, walking in all the commandments
and ordinances of the Lord blameless. (Luke 1:6)

Elizabeth faced an extremely difficult challenge in her life: she was childless. In her culture, this could only mean that God was withholding His blessing because of His displeasure. Her barren state was there for the world to see—and to gossip about. It is likely that Elizabeth faced a great deal of criticism and rebuke to get her life right with the Lord. But in reality, her life *was* right with Him.

Elizabeth walked blamelessly before the Lord and was even described as righteous. She remained obedient in all things. It was because of her faithfulness that God entrusted Elizabeth with the son about whom Jesus later said, "Among those born of women there is not a greater prophet than John the Baptist" (Luke 7:28). Elizabeth would also be used to encourage her young cousin Mary, who would give birth to Jesus, God's Son.

Elizabeth was steadfast in the face of great discouragement and suffering over her childlessness and cultural disgrace. Yet nothing was more important than pleasing her Lord—and He honored her daily faithfulness to Him!

We lived each day trusting that God would provide, that He would build His church, and that He would reveal His plans for us. Taking things one step at a time kept us from being overwhelmed with the challenges we faced. Everything hinged on our daily walk with the Lord.

> *"Obey My voice, and I will be your God, and you shall be My people. And walk in all the ways that I have commanded you, that it may be well with you."*
> —*Jeremiah 7:23*

OBEDIENCE THROUGH DIFFICULTIES

The early days in Saskatoon were extremely difficult. The children went through enormous changes as they adjusted to the culture and the school system. Our older boys were expected to have well-developed skills in such sports as ice skating and hockey—skills the boys in Saskatoon had mastered at much younger ages. This put them at a disadvantage. Making friends in the middle of the school year was also tough, and the support and friendships they had been used to at our church in California weren't available at this church. The only other children in the church at the time were part of a family from the States who had come to work with us. They helped us a great deal, drawing people to the church through music, but unfortunately, the dark and frigid winters of Saskatoon became too much for them, and they returned home after 10 months.

Meanwhile, Henry was working hard in ministry. He led not only our church but also several new church plants in the surrounding areas. Most of the time, I would play the piano or organ for the worship time while Henry preached and led the people in worship. In the beginning, we would have our Sunday school and worship service and then drive two hours to another town, where we led another Sunday school and service. We would return in time for the evening worship service at our church. Then after the service, we had a fellowship time in the home of a church member, where we had discipleship training and a light supper. It was a grueling schedule for all of us, and eventually I stayed home with the kids instead of traveling to the other church service 90 miles away.

On weekday evenings, Henry often led Bible studies in different towns and cities where there was no evangelical witness. We weren't always welcomed with open arms, and one group even took out a full-page ad in the local paper to protest a church God had led our congregation to start in the town. In California, I had been accustomed to being part of a successful ministry in which people often responded to the Lord. We had seen amazing works of God in the prisons and with the gangs around the San Francisco area, and we were used to regularly witnessing the miracle of changed lives. I thought of myself as a pleasant and friendly person whose husband was an accomplished and effective speaker. Yet after more than two years of hard, exhausting work, we had only 35 people in our Saskatoon church.

It was especially discouraging for my oldest son. One Sunday, he came up to me and said, "Mom, I feel so sorry for Dad. He preaches his heart out every Sunday, and no one comes forward to respond." I mentioned this to Henry right away, and he took Richard aside and told him, "It's enough that God chose to use us at all; it isn't the response that shows whether we're successful, but if our lives please the Lord" (2 Corinthians 5:9).

What was difficult to see in those demanding early days was that God was indeed working, and He was using this time to prepare His people to experience Him. Although God's activity wasn't always visible, He was always at work around us. It was toward the end of our second year that we really saw Him start to move with power.

When we arrived in Saskatoon, Henry had joined a group of interdenominational pastors in the city who had been meeting every week for prayer. For one and a half years, they united in prayer for God to bring revival. In time, God began to stir in the hearts of the Christians to repent and return to Him, and revival came to Saskatoon. Services were held at Ebenezer Baptist Church, but before very long, the building couldn't hold all the people who came. Services were then moved to St. Timothy's Anglican Church, but that only lasted one evening, and we had to move to the larger sanctuary of the University Drive Alliance Church. Two days later, the revival services were conducted in the largest sanctuary in the city, Third Avenue United Church, and the nightly gatherings lasted for seven and a half weeks.

Although we have no recorded numbers of those who decided to follow Christ during the revival, we saw remarkable and miraculous changes in the city of Saskatoon. The newspaper reported that people who had stolen things from Sears throughout the years made so many store returns that profits were soaring. The Canadian Revenue Agency testified that people were calling and sending in money for falsely reporting their tax returns in the past. It was a miraculous time that is still remembered today. In fact, Henry and

LOTTIE MOON
(1840–1912)

One of the most famous missionaries in Baptist circles is Charlotte Diggs Moon. She was born to a wealthy Virginia plantation owner and had a rich heritage of faith. Her mother greatly influenced the family toward missions and serving others. Lottie's two older sisters were also involved in missions, and at 33, the attractive Lottie left a promising and comfortable future to serve in North China with her sister.

After a difficult journey, she realized that God had entrusted her with a special assignment for which no personal sacrifice could be too great. She devoted herself to learning the Chinese language and culture. After her sister became ill and returned home, Lottie continued to minister as a counselor, guide, preacher, and teacher to countless women and children. She pioneered work in unreached villages, traveling for days on a mule. "Never angry, never impatient, never resentful, she patiently wore away the prejudices and hatred by her gentle, gracious presence and her blameless life."[1] Even in hostile places, she was known as "the foreign lady with the big love heart." Lottie survived severe poverty, revolutions, war, smallpox, and the plague, but she finally died of starvation on Christmas Eve, 1912. Her pleas for support began the annual mission offering, called the Lottie Moon Christmas Offering, which, to this day, supports thousands of missionaries around the world.[2]

I recently attended the 35-year anniversary celebration of the revival that God brought about in Saskatoon.

Even though the numbers remained small at our church, it was through this citywide revival that the foundation of our church was built. Our little congregation of 35 didn't want to settle for less than what the Lord had planned for us, and we were actively seeking where God wanted us to be involved. We spent time together each week as a church family to see what God was doing and what He revealed to the members.

After the initial challenges of those first few years, God blessed our continued obedience and commitment to Him. Our numbers grew, new ministries were launched, and a theological school was founded to train church leaders. We also started new churches in two other provinces and saw many people come to know the Lord.

> *"As the Father loved Me, I also have loved you; abide in My love. If you keep My commandments, you will abide in My love, just as I have kept My Father's commandments and abide in His love. These things I have spoken to you, that My joy may remain in you, and that your joy may be full."*
> *—John 15:9–11*

DAILY OBEDIENCE COMES FROM A LOVE RELATIONSHIP

As I've said before, it became very clear to us that if we hadn't gone to Saskatoon because we loved God and wanted to obey Him (John

14:7, 21, 23), we would not have seen Him at work the way we did.

For some people, daily obedience is a discipline that has to be cultivated. Having spiritual discipline is a good thing, but having discipline without a love relationship can degenerate into legalism. When you love someone, you want to spend time with him or her. In my relationship with Henry, I can't love him only part of the time; I have to love him all the time and trust him in our relationship. It is even more so with our Lord. God looks past all our good works, our struggle to be disciplined, and our time spent on church-related functions, and He searches our hearts to see if we love Him. If we love Him, we will want to obey Him in all He instructs (John 14:15). Following the Lord in obedience because we love Him will lead to a deep and meaningful relationship with Him through which He will work to bless and reach others.

> *But his delight is in the law of the LORD, and in His law he meditates day and night. He shall be like a tree planted by the rivers of water, that brings forth its fruit in its season, whose leaf also shall not wither; and whatever he does shall prosper.*
> *—Psalm 1:2–3*

THE COST OF OBEDIENCE

The number-one question people have asked me at the many conferences we've done over the years is "How do you deal with the cost of following the Lord?" Frankly, it is easy to come up with many justifications as to why we can't obey what God wants us to do:

- We would have to leave our relatives.
- Our kids would struggle with adjustments.
- It would create stress or problems at work.
- We don't feel ready.
- The weather is too cold, or there isn't enough sunshine where God wants us to go.
- It's not what we were trained for.
- Not enough money is provided.
- We're just plain afraid of change.

Every person has a different reason. When people request my advice about how they should handle what God has told them in light of all these other obstacles, I simply ask, "What did God say when you told Him all of your concerns?"

When we turn our focus to the Lord and all He has done for us and wants to do for us and through us in the future, the excuses are small details to be dealt with. In fact, for us to disobey our Lord, who saved us and called us into relationship with Him, is unimaginable. Some who place the cost above their obedience don't realize that there is a higher price to pay for disobedience, such as never knowing how God could have used them, not understanding the impact their obedience could have made on their own families, missing out on a deeper relationship with the Lord that comes from trusting Him to guide, and not experiencing the deep joy of stepping out in faith and pleasing the Lord.

But perhaps the greatest cost is realizing that people whose lives could have been changed forever because of our obedience may never come to know the love of Christ. God may use other means to reach the people He wanted to impact through our lives, but those particular opportunities for us to be involved in His activity will pass us by. God allows us to be involved in His activity for our sake, so we can know Him better and experience the joy of being part of His work. God can use anything or anyone to touch another person's life or to further His activity, so when the honor comes to us, we shouldn't let it pass us by.

Roll your works upon the Lord [commit and trust them wholly to Him; He will cause your thoughts to become agreeable to His will, and] so shall your plans be established and succeed.
—*Proverbs 16:3 (AMP)*

SETTLING OR OBEYING

I came to a point in my life where I was truly willing to live the rest of my life in Saskatoon. We had been there 12 years, and we had made the parsonage quite livable. I had made some very nice curtains for the windows, we finally had carpet on the floors, and we had installed a second bathroom in the basement. I had even discovered that our broken-down car, which was stuck in our driveway, made the best freezer all winter long—and it had plenty of space for frozen food. Life was looking great!

It was in the midst of this contentment that Henry and I felt God calling us to a new type of ministry. Henry had received a phone call about a new position in which he was really needed:

director of missions for the Capilano Association in Vancouver, British Columbia. We had never before considered anything but the pastorate.

We knew that if we moved to Vancouver at this point, we would have to leave our two oldest children in Saskatoon to finish university. This was hard for me! As I was talking to the Lord, He clearly asked me if I would rather stay with what I knew or if I would rather go with what He wanted to give me. This ended the discussion, because I knew I would rather go with what God had in store for me than settle for what was comfortable.

I have never forgotten God's question, nor have I ever regretted my answer. It was our denominational work in Vancouver that eventually led Henry to work for the Home Mission Board in Atlanta, Georgia (now known as the North American Mission Board), and serve with people who encouraged him to write *Experiencing God*. It's amazing how God used so many steps of obedience to lead us to where our lives are today. I have often wondered what would have happened if we had chosen to stay in Saskatoon, and I thank God every day that He gave me the choice to obey Him.

THE BENEFITS OF DAILY OBEDIENCE

Because God is all-knowing, He is able to prepare us for things we will face not only in our own lives but in the world around us. Just as Jesus prepared the disciples for His death—although they didn't understand until much later—God chooses to help us.

Whenever God was about to do something in the Old Testament, He told someone who was walking closely with Him. When He was going to destroy the earth with a flood, He told Noah (Genesis 6:7–8, 13, 17). When God was about to destroy Sodom and Gomorrah, He told Abraham (Genesis 18:16–33). When God was ready to deliver His people from slavery, He told Moses (Exodus 3:7–10). When the Lord intended to give Israel a king, He revealed it to Samuel (1 Samuel 16:1–13). Scripture is filled with numerous examples of God preparing those who walk closely with Him for future events, and His ways have not changed.

> *"However, when He, the Spirit of truth, has come,*
> *He will guide you into all truth; for He will not*
> *speak on His own authority, but whatever He hears*
> *He will speak; and He will tell you things to come."*
> —*John 16:13*

A SHAKEN FOUNDATION

After living in Atlanta for several years, working for the North American Mission Board, Henry retired and we started a new ministry that allowed him to write and share what God placed on his heart. It was during this time that we experienced God's preparation for a time of crisis.

For several days in 2001, Psalm 11:3 continually came to Henry and me: "If the foundations are destroyed, what can the righteous do?" We didn't understand why this verse was being impressed on our hearts, but we did feel that God was preparing us to have our foundations shaken in some way. Later that week, we attended our ministry's semiannual board meeting, held at the Chick-fil-A headquarters in Atlanta, to discuss the details of the work and to make plans for the future.

Henry would always begin the meetings with a devotional thought, and that morning, he shared what God had been saying to us: "When our foundation is shaken, when everything we know is being turned upside down, we need to stay close to the Lord and continue to obey His voice. God is still on His throne no matter what the situation we face, and when He speaks, we need to pay attention."

In the middle of the devotion, a secretary entered the room and whispered something to one of our board members. I could tell the news was terribly upsetting, but he didn't want to interrupt. After a few minutes, I stopped Henry and asked the man what was wrong. He told us that the World Trade Center had been hit by a plane.

Soon, more people were entering the room to let the other board members know what was happening. We were all stunned. While we were listening to a message about our foundations being shaken, our world was changing before our eyes, never to be the same again.

Truett Cathy, the founder of Chick-fil-A, heard that Henry was in the building and asked if he would pray for the nation with all the employees. Gathering together in the atrium to voice our prayers to the Lord for His comfort and direction in this moment of crisis was an unforgettable experience.

See that you do not refuse Him who speaks. For if they did not escape who refused Him who spoke on earth, much more shall we not escape if we turn away from Him who speaks from heaven, whose voice then shook the earth; but now He has promised, saying, "Yet once more I shake not only the earth, but also heaven." Now this, "Yet once more," indicates the removal of those things that are being shaken, as of things that are made, that the things which cannot be shaken may remain. Therefore, since we are receiving a kingdom which cannot be shaken, let us have grace, by which we may serve God acceptably with reverence and godly fear. For our God is a consuming fire.
—Hebrews 12:25–29

If we daily seek the Lord, He will prepare us for the situations we will face (see Matthew 2:13–20). We probably won't know all the facts, but when the crisis comes, we can adjust and continue to obey the Lord. When we remain focused on Him through reading Scripture and praying, we will have God's power to endure any struggle.

Our nature is frail and flawed, yet when we allow Jesus to live out His life through us—through our daily obedience to Him—we can always remain in His will because we will always have ready access to God's wisdom and grace (Luke 1:37, Hebrews 4:16). When we're fellowshipping daily with Him, He prepares us in advance for many of the difficulties we face. A devotional or Scripture passage we read one morning may focus our thoughts on a truth we'll need that afternoon. Or our prayer time may lead us to pray for our children, who will later face a temptation and need wisdom or direction.

When we're empowered by the Lord through our time with Him, nothing we experience will exceed God's wisdom or ability to help us through.

> *"You are My friends if you do whatever I command*
> *you. No longer do I call you servants, for a*
> *servant does not know what his master is doing;*
> *but I have called you friends, for all things that*
> *I heard from My Father I have made known to*
> *you. You did not choose Me, but I chose you."*
> —*John 15:14–16*

PLACING GOD FIRST

When we make the commitment to place God first in our lives, each step we take will be filled with a joy that comes from Him. If we truly love the Lord, we'll want to obey and please Him; disobedience tells God we don't love Him (John 14:23–24). Any half measures or partial efforts aren't worthy of the Lord we serve.

Life can be hard. It brings challenges and struggles and crises we must face, but it was never meant to be something we have to walk through alone. God desires a daily relationship with us in which we will grow ever deeper in love and trust. He wants us to succeed, and He gives us the ability to know His will so that when we obey Him, our efforts will always accomplish what He intended. He also provides a never-ending resource of power for us to draw from, so when the difficult times inevitably come, we won't have to face burnout while serving Him. It's our responsibility to draw daily from that source so that we'll be prepared for the challenges ahead. If we lack wisdom, or any good thing, we simply need to turn to the Lord and ask. Serving the Lord in our own strength will lead to burnout and discouragement. However, in God's power, we can accomplish anything He asks of us.

One of my favorite quotes in the updated edition of *Experiencing God* comes from George Müller, who had a powerful relationship with the Lord:

> I never remember . . . a period . . . that I ever sincerely and
> patiently sought to know the will of God by the teaching of
> the Holy Ghost, through the instrumentality of the Word of
> God, but I have been always directed rightly. But if honesty of
> heart and uprightness before God were lacking or if I did not
> patiently wait upon God for instruction, or if I preferred the
> counsel of my fellow men to the declarations of the Word of
> the living God, I made great mistakes.[3]

QUESTIONS FOR DEEPER REFLECTION

1. Following the Lord is both a choice made at the beginning of our relationship with Him as well as a daily choice we make as we live our lives. Each small step of obedience is important and will lead to a fuller and more meaningful relationship with

the Lord. Can you remember a time when you clearly identi-
fied God directing your life? If so, what was the result of your
obedience or disobedience? If you can't remember a time when
you felt God directing you, pray with the commitment to
obey, asking God to show you what He would have you do.

2. When we look at the examples of Lottie Moon and John the
Baptist's mother, Elizabeth, we can be both inspired and
influenced by their obedience and dedication to the Lord.
Studying the lives of people God has used in the past is
important in understanding how He deals with us today. I
would challenge you to read a book about a man or woman
God has used for His mighty purposes and allow it to challenge your own life and walk with the Lord.

3. God uses our daily time with Him to prepare us for what
we will face in the future. He has given us many examples
in Scripture, and He continues to function this way. How
have you felt that God has prepared you for all you've
experienced? Can you identify a time that God provided
you with the answers to questions you have later faced?
God not only has wisdom for any situation; He also promises to give us wisdom if we diligently seek Him (Proverbs
2:6, 7; 3:13; 4:5–7; 8:1–17*; 16:20; 19:8). We encourage
you to read a chapter from Proverbs each day during your
time with the Lord. Since there are 31, it's easy to keep track.
God won't withhold guidance from us when we truly seek to
obey Him.

* This is one of the key chapters on wisdom in Proverbs.

QUESTIONS FOR GROUP DISCUSSION

1. How would you characterize your relationship with the Lord? Would you view your relationship with Him as dynamic, exciting, and joyful? Or do you lean more toward words like empty, routine, or a struggle? Take time to reflect together on all the Lord has done: how He has changed your lives, and how He has worked through each of you and expressed His deep love for you. Share some of those experiences.

2. Encouraging one another in our daily walk is one of God's blessings to us. Watching Him work through prayer or seeing a friend overcome a stumbling block is exciting. How can you be more proactive in encouraging those around you? Share some of those ideas.

4

HOMEMAKER OR MISSIONARY

"For My thoughts are not your thoughts, nor are your ways My ways," says the LORD. "For as the heavens are higher than the earth, so are My ways higher than your ways, and My thoughts than your thoughts."
—Isaiah 55:8–9

Never-ending cleaning, vacuuming, doing dishes, washing clothes, ironing, changing sheets, seemingly constant cooking for four (or more) boys . . . Was this the work of a missionary?

I had idyllic childhood dreams of what the life of a missionary would be like. I had visions of riding a burro over stony mountain passes to spread the love of Jesus to unreached people groups in South America. I envisioned learning to balance a basket on my head while sharing the good news of Jesus Christ with African women. I even had dreams of flying around the world as an airline flight attendant, spreading the gospel to all those stuck on the plane with me. Whatever I was to do, I knew that it was going to be exciting and that God would work powerfully through my life to impact all those around me—and, of course, many people would come to know Jesus!

As an adult, I learned the difference between my childhood dreams and the reality of living a life of servanthood. My exciting adventures turned into less-than-thrilling housework, and I struggled between my call from the Lord to missions and the actuality of my everyday life. I saw my husband involved in God's work—helping people grow spiritually, starting churches and Bible studies, and even founding a theological school to train and equip people for ministry. And what was my task? Housework. Never-ending housework! This wasn't what I had imagined when I thought of mission work, and it was discouraging.

I couldn't see how my life was making a difference and impacting the people around me. One day while I was vacuuming and talking to the Lord, I simply asked Him, "Is this the work of a missionary? Cooking? Cleaning? Laundry?" The answer was clear and life changing for me. He simply spoke to my heart, "Yes, this is the work I have for you right now."

Knowing that I was obeying the Lord and pleasing Him changed my perspective and lightened my heart. Soon, serving the Lord in seemingly mundane tasks renewed my joy. As my attitude changed, opportunities to minister to others in my home came, and I saw God at work in a fresh way. I wasn't simply the unpaid cleaning staff. God had a purpose for me and for what I was doing, and I needed to stay alert to His activity and look for the opportunities He would bring.

> *But Jesus said, "Let the little children come to Me, and do not forbid them; for of such is the kingdom of heaven."*
> *—Matthew 19:14*

DISGUISED OPPORTUNITIES

God had placed an enormous responsibility in my hands: my children. But He not only gave me my children to guide and influence (Genesis 17:7; Deuteronomy 6:7); He also assigned to me all the kids on the block, who loved to play in our yard.

Through those early years, we received a lot of criticism from the neighborhood for our terrible-looking yard. No matter what kind of fertilizer we used, our grass had bald patches where the kids played soccer and every other sport they could think of. Our flowers were unintentionally trampled by kids chasing soccer balls or footballs. The kids were constantly jumping over our newly planted pine trees, which had been planted to help beautify the yard. Every winter we would water our backyard garden, creating a wonderful ice rink where all the kids came to play hockey—but leaving a huge mess in the spring.

God revealed an opportunity for ministry right in our own yard (John 4:35). Every day, children from up and down the street played at our house. God opened my eyes, and I decided that if kids played in my yard, I could share the love of Jesus with them. I began to make cinnamon rolls and snacks for them, all the while singing and sharing stories about Jesus. But more importantly, I was simply showing love to kids who came home from school to empty houses, or kids who felt lonely, unloved, or unwanted. I was the "block mom" to many of the children (Matthew 18:5). Yes, I worked harder in the home than I ever had before. But through the years, God allowed me to see almost all of those kids come to our church and our youth group, and even see them come to a saving relationship with Christ. God had a plan to use me in the home. I could have done many other types of ministry—women's ministry, Bible studies, prayer ministry—but in the end, nothing was more important than the children God brought into my life.

BLESSINGS AND REGRETS

There were two boys in particular whom God placed in my life. Their mother had left them on the first day of their first- and

KATHERINE VON BORA
(1499–1552)

Katherine had a noble heritage, and after her mother's death, she was sent to an upper-class convent to live. There she learned farming, German, and Latin, as well as the meaning of prayer.[1] As Martin Luther's reformation against the Catholic Church began, it spread into the convents and monasteries. Katherine, along with several others, sought to leave the order to pursue God's salvation outside of their isolation. Eventually turning to Martin Luther for help, they made a daring escape.

Katherine made it clear that she wanted to marry Martin Luther because of his faith, and eventually, Luther decided to marry "his beloved Kate." Although sharply criticized for his decision to marry, Luther commented, "I would not change my Katie for France and Venice, because God has given her to me, and she is true to me and a good mother to my children."[2]

Katherine embodied the example in Proverbs 31. Luther safely trusted his wife with his household and children. She was full of energy and worked hard to provide food for all who stayed with them, including six other children she raised and students and boarders from the university. She worked with her hands, kept a clean house, taught her children well, was an able doctor, and was wise in the Scriptures. Luther later said that he "thanked God for his pious and true wife on whom a husband's heart can rely."[3]

third-grade years, and they were devastated. My heart broke as I watched them struggle, and I decided to help them in any way I could. They lived across the street from us and were regularly a part of our mealtimes—so much so that their father even offered to give me money for groceries. We loved these boys and became involved in their lives. Although, initially, their father didn't want the boys to go to church with us, he relented when he saw the positive influence of our family and the difference it made in the lives of his sons. Through the years, I watched these two boys learn from their mistakes and eventually come to a saving relationship with the Lord.

When the time came for us to move to Vancouver, we left our two oldest boys in Saskatoon to finish university. It was hard to leave our kids, but it was also difficult for me to leave the two boys from across the street, whom I'd loved as my own children. Since both were young adults by this time, I thought they would be happy not to have me looking over their shoulders, making sure they were eating properly and staying out of trouble.

I didn't realize until later that our move had had a deep impact on these boys, almost as if their mother had left them again. Henry and I didn't have much money, and phone calls were expensive. We also didn't have a computer or e-mail, and writing letters was time consuming and slow. Not realizing how important it was, I didn't take the time. When we called our sons, I always tried to talk to the other two boys whenever they were there, but catching everyone at home at the same time was impossible. If I could do it all over again, I would have made sure the boys knew they would always have a place in our family by taking the time to write letters and calling specifically to talk to them. Although both boys finished university

and have done well, I can't help but think that I could have continued to be a positive influence in their lives. Nurturing doesn't end
when children leave home—or in our case, when we leave them at
home—it continues for a lifetime. It may look and feel different as
the years pass, but making the extra effort to stay involved (even if
they don't seem to want it) can provide the stability they need to
have the courage to follow the Lord on their own adventure.

> *And whatever you do, do it heartily, as to the Lord and not
> to men, knowing that from the Lord you will receive the
> reward of the inheritance; for you serve the Lord Christ.*
> — *Colossians 3:23–24*

SPENDING TIME WISELY

Everywhere I go, people ask, "How on earth did you find time to
spend time with the Lord when you had so many small children?"

I had all five children within nine and a half years, so finding
time with the Lord was extremely challenging. When the children
were young, having a break meant taking a nap! With five very
active children, all in different stages of development, I never had
an idle moment to escape somewhere by myself.

I found that if I wanted to have my time with the Lord, especially
in the early days, I had to be creative. I also had to multitask. For me,
quality time was more important (and more realistic) than quantity
time. I found I could spread out my time with the Lord throughout
the day and still learn and grow in my relationship with Him. I became skilled at concentrating while on the move. I found that I could

talk to God at least a good solid hour, although often interrupted with different crises, while I did the required vacuuming, ironing, and cleaning for a household of seven. Some of my most memorable conversations with the Lord happened while I was vacuuming.

> *The wise woman builds her house, but the*
> *foolish pulls it down with her hands.*
> *— Proverbs 14:1*

WATCHING MY ATTITUDE

Placing a priority on having time with the Lord, even if it was while I was washing dishes, helped me keep my attitude and perspective focused on Him. As a mother, I found that my children would usually reflect my attitude and feelings about something. Whether I was positive or negative, my attitude had an enormous effect on the entire household. This was especially true with respect to my husband. I learned early on that whatever thoughts and feelings I had regarding my husband's constant absence because of the ministry were echoed by my children. If I was resentful, they were resentful. If I was sure he was doing what God wanted him to do and I was proud of how God was using him, the children would often express

> *It was my job to bridge the gap between my hardworking husband and the children who wanted to know him.*

the same feelings when my husband came home. There is nothing worse than sullen looks and disapproval from a wife when her husband comes home from a hard day. I didn't want that kind of atmosphere for myself, my husband, or my children.

What I discovered, es-pecially while the children were young, was that my outlook set the tone for the entire household. It was my job to bridge the gap between my hardworking husband and the children who wanted to know him (Proverbs 31:11–12). It was my responsibility to teach our children to respect their father and what God had called him to do—and, ultimately, what God had called us to do as a family.

> *I call to remembrance the genuine faith*
> *that is in you, which dwelt first in your*
> *grandmother Lois and your mother Eunice,*
> *and I am persuaded is in you also.*
> —2 Timothy 1:5

CAN HOMEMAKING BE A CALLING?

One day my husband and I were speaking at a conference, and a pastor's wife came to me in tears, seeking my advice. She had a new baby and really enjoyed staying home to care for her. The problem was that her maternity leave was almost up, and it was tearing her apart to think about going back to work. She didn't know what to do.

Unfortunately, this situation isn't unusual. Often a lack of income prompts women to work outside the home to help provide for the family. That was what this pastor's wife was facing. I sat down to talk with her and simply asked her what God wanted her to do with her life. She gave me a strange look and asked what I meant. "Does God want you to stay home with your child, or does He want you to go back to work?" I asked. This fundamental question is often overlooked.

It isn't a question of how much money we need to pay next month's bills. It isn't a question of how we can best be fulfilled in our lives. Nor is it a question that should be answered on the basis of our emotions alone. The issue for all of us is simply, "What does God want us to do?"

I told this mother to spend some time with the Lord to find out what He wanted for her and her family. Only He knew the answer to this question, and neither logical deduction nor a pros-and-cons list would help. She told me that she really believed God wanted her to stay home with her child, and then she asked for advice about how to do that.

I talked with this young mother about her financial situation and offered a suggestion: Learn to do without. For her and her family, that meant doing without a second car and the corresponding insurance payments, which were killing them financially. Since her husband's job allowed her to drop him off and keep the car during the day, they decided to sell both of their cars and buy a family vehicle that was more cost-efficient. Now that she was no longer working outside the home, the family saved a great deal of money by not eating out so often. I also helped her plan a weekly menu and shopping list so the family was not only saving money but eating healthy. And because she wasn't going to the office, she saved a lot of money on work clothes, nylons, and shoes. These combined factors made up the financial difference from her job. She was so excited! She began to experience the joy that comes from obeying God and being in the center of His will. I checked on her several months later, and she was doing well.

God has a plan for each one of us (Jeremiah 29:11–13). For many, that plan will be to make their home the priority—especially while their children are younger. For others God's plan may be for them to use their gifts in the workplace. Regardless of whether you serve the Lord at home or in the workforce, He wants you to make a difference where He has placed you. The key is to understand what God's plan is for you and obey—regardless of the cost.

> *She watches over the ways of her household,*
> *and does not eat the bread of idleness.*
> *Her children rise up and call her blessed;*
> *her husband also, and he praises her.*
> *— Proverbs 31:27–28*

WHAT IS A HOMEMAKER?

For many women today, the word *homemaker* is seen as a negative term. It conjures up thoughts that I described earlier—images of cleaning, cooking, washing dishes, doing laundry, ironing, vacuuming, and other onerous household tasks. Yet that isn't what a homemaker is. These chores must be done in every household, regardless of whether you work at home or in the marketplace. A homemaker is what the word implies: home maker.

MARTHA

Jesus came to Bethany, where Lazarus was who had
been dead, whom He had raised from the dead. There they
made Him a supper; and Martha served (John 12:1–2).

Martha was a very special person in the life of Jesus. She was the keeper of the home where Jesus liked to stay, enjoy a meal, and teach His disciples. She sought to serve the Lord and give Him her best.

Through Martha, we are given a wonderful scriptural example of the love that Jesus has for His followers—a love that doesn't leave us where we are but takes us to where we should be.

John 11:5 tells of Jesus' love for Martha and her family. He had spent time with them and knew them well. He raised Martha's brother, Lazarus, from the dead to help them see that He was the resurrection and the life. Martha, however, didn't fully understand what Jesus was trying to teach her. She, like a good homemaker, was seeking to provide for her guests as she always did. Busy, busy, busy! She most likely took great pride in her work, yet her focus was on her work, not her relationship with Jesus. Jesus didn't condemn Martha for her desire to serve, but He reminded her that while He was there, it was necessary to put other things aside and experience Him. Martha must have understood, for the next time Jesus came, she was serving with joy. Busyness can never replace time with the Lord.

Being a homemaker isn't just cleaning the house; it's making a home for your family. There are many different ways we can create a home environment for our families. For generations, women have worked with their hands. I learned to sew out of necessity to provide clothing for my family, but it has become a real joy to me over the years. Currently, a special group of women meets weekly in my home for a time of fellowship and fun while we work on different projects.

As I said earlier, my sewing ability opened up a mission opportunity teaching Cambodian women how to smock to supplement their families' income. We recently learned how important this project has been. Even medical teams are being restricted from places that are hostile to Christianity. But apparently, a trade is looked upon as a valuable skill that Christians can teach to people in countries leery of Christianity.

> *Being a homemaker isn't just cleaning the house; it's making a home for your family.*

I also cross-stitched a scripture passage for each one of my children. It is my hope that this will help them remember the importance of God's Word and how much I care about their spiritual welfare.

But being a homemaker isn't about sewing or knitting or quilting or cross-stitching, nor is this role exclusive to stay-at-home moms. Every woman is a homemaker, whether or not she has children, whether she works inside or outside the home, whether or not she has a university degree, whether she is rich or poor, whether she is married or single. In most situations, women set the tone for the home. Regardless of your circumstances, it's important to see how you can have a positive impact on your family and do the best job with the time you have.

Find what you enjoy and use your abilities to create a loving atmosphere at home. Gardening, cooking, decorating, carpooling, hiding notes in lunch boxes, hosting game nights, baking cookies—any interest that facilitates a warm and caring environment and directs your family toward the love of God is what being a homemaker is all about. Look for creative ways to encourage and build relationships in your home and see the difference it makes for your husband, your children, and yourself. Your home will be a place not only where your own family wants to be, but where friends and neighbors will want to congregate as well.

Opportunities to make a difference in others' lives often come by opening up your home to others. Sharing ourselves and doing what we love to do with our families, looking for opportunities to encourage others, taking the time to pay attention to the small things—these are essential aspects of being a homemaker. Yes, for most of us, cooking and cleaning and laundry are part of our responsibilities. But excellent housekeeping, sewing, baking, or even ironing doesn't necessarily make us good homemakers. When we are seeking to create a home for our families, we are limited only by our creativity and imagination.

Therefore, whether you eat or drink,
or whatever you do, do all to the glory of God.
—1 Corinthians 10:31

WHEN THERE IS ONLY ONE OPTION

Knowing what God intends for us—understanding His will—and then doing it with all our hearts should always be most important in our lives. This will look different for each believer. God, in His wonderful plan, made each of us unique. There is no cookie-cutter pattern that makes one woman better than another. Each woman is responsible to be obedient to what God has called her to do.

For some, especially those who find themselves raising their children alone, staying at home is not an option. From the time I was 16, I always had a job and worked hard paying my way through school. When I married, I chose to stop working outside the home and start a family. But as I've said before, while we were serving the Lord in Saskatoon, our church couldn't pay us an adequate salary. I remember going for an entire month without a penny to buy groceries. I became very creative. My younger children never had anything but powdered milk, and they even joked with other kids that their milk came from a blender instead of a cow! Despite being frugal, we eventually accumulated some debt, and there seemed to be no way for us to pay it off with our meager mission's wages. I knew that to get back into the black, I had to find a paying job. There was nothing else we could cut back on to save more money.

Since all my children were in school at this point, I began looking for a day job that would allow me to be home in the evenings. I looked everywhere! I either had too much education (which made it too expensive to hire me) or other applicants had more recent experience. Finally, God gave me a job in a rest home, which provided the opportunity for me to work with the medical community and spend time with lonely people who needed a listening ear.

It was challenging to work full time and try to keep up with my responsibilities at home, but God provided the strength and the patience when I asked for it. He also helped me place my weariness from work aside, giving me energy when I returned to my family after an exhausting day.

Over the years, God provided for our needs in many other ways: I provided childcare for another mother, sold my china painting, gardened, and made deals with local farmers for fresh meat and produce. My older boys would sometimes go out early in the mornings to duck hunt. We had many a meal with buckshot in it! God also provided each of our children with jobs that helped them get through college and seminary completely debt-free.

When our children were young, my husband and I prayed that God would either bless us financially or help our children to not realize how poor we were. We didn't want them to grow up with a "poor" mentality. Although I'm sure the children would have preferred for us to have more money, the Lord blinded them to what they didn't have. Looking back, although we always worked hard to make ends meet, God provided us with the necessities, and none of our children ever went without what they really needed (Psalm 37:25).

Several years after I had worked at the rest home, I learned that my time in the workplace had a benefit beyond just the physical provision for our family. God used the two years I worked with the medical community at the rest home to prepare me for understanding the doctors and their terminology as well as the care needed for my daughter when she became seriously ill. God used all of these experiences in my life to help me grow in my faith, trusting in His daily guidance. He showed me the importance of my time with Him: to give me the physical and spiritual resources to get me through the day. God starts with us where we are and uses the circumstances around us to build our character so that we will become more like Christ.

> *"This is My commandment, that you*
> *love one another as I have loved you."*
> —John 15:12

BEING A HOMEMAKER IS A LIFELONG TASK

We must know God's direction for our lives. Regardless of our education, background, or financial situation, God can use us to be a stabilizing factor in our homes. When we know that God is with us and has a plan for our lives, we can handle anything thrown at us. He doesn't promise that life will be easy, but He does promise to walk with us through each situation.

For everything there is a season (Ecclesiastes 3:1). Assignments change and enlarge as we obey God and as our love for Him grows. I have had many different seasons in my life as a homemaker and many different experiences both in the home and in the workforce. God has given me opportunities to work alongside my husband, speaking and traveling and meeting new people. And in this season of my life I'm enjoying my 14 grandchildren. God didn't have a career in the workplace for me. My lifetime job has been and still is helping my husband and providing a home where he can have some peace and rest.

Being a homemaker is always an interesting yet challenging assignment. My husband was recently extremely ill, and since then I have needed to learn a whole new way of cooking to keep him healthy and prepared for whatever God calls him to do next. I have learned many things about grinding wheat for bread, cooking without preservatives, and finding ways to lower our sugar intake. My husband knows that I love him enough to learn new things and to change old habits to give him a better life. He is my responsibility, as I am his. Every morning, after spending time with the Lord, Henry brings me my first cup of coffee and tells me what God has shared with him. We share a pilgrimage with the Lord, and we walk together. We each have our part to fulfill.

Again, when thinking about being a homemaker, we shouldn't just think of it as simply cleaning the house, cooking the meals, and making pretty things for the walls. God can use everything we do to make our marriage and our home a peaceful and spiritual place. Making the best use of time, looking for opportunities to talk to the Lord, creating ways to direct our children to the right path, seeking to build that bridge between a busy husband and our children, creating a welcoming environment for guests—these things aren't easy! They aren't for the fainthearted. Homemaking *is* a full-time job!

Although being a homemaker may sometimes seem like a thankless responsibility, ultimately, we're seeking to please the Lord. There is a spiritual reward coming that we cannot see yet, and I think a large portion is reserved for homemakers! Also, watching our spouses or children venture out into the world with confidence, knowing they can return to a loving and encouraging home, is a reward of its own. Our satisfaction comes not from the praise of people but from the Lord. For the tasks we do are God-given, and our job is to please Him! If we are always looking to glorify the Lord, He will honor all that we do in His time.

> *We . . . do not cease to pray for you, and to ask that you may be filled with the knowledge of His will in all wisdom and spiritual understanding; that you may walk worthy of the Lord, fully pleasing Him, being fruitful in every good work and increasing in the knowledge of God.*
> *—Colossians 1:9–10*

QUESTIONS FOR DEEPER REFLECTION

1. Being a homemaker is a multifaceted job. It requires hard work, creativity, sensitivity, energy, and, I think, a sense of humor. How have you viewed the term *homemaker* in the past? Has God opened your eyes to any new aspects of what it means to be a homemaker? Take some time to reflect on what makes you successful as a homemaker, as well as any changes you need to make in this area.

2. Taking time with the Lord, no matter how brief, is essential in the Christian's life. Evaluate how you spend your time. Finding an hour in the morning or evening might be impos-

sible at this stage in your life, but praying while folding laundry or washing dishes is better than spending no time with the Lord at all. I encourage you to identify a few times in the day when you will make God a priority, even if it's for only a few minutes at a time while you're doing other things. Write your commitment down and see how God can help you structure your day.

3. Our attitude is so important in all we do. Although Martha was doing good things, she was caught up in the busyness instead of focusing on the moments she could have spent with the Lord (see Luke 10:38–42). It is our attitude in service that God is looking for, not the number of our accomplishments. Have you been goal- or work-oriented? Do you serve with a cheerful heart? Take some time to examine your attitude and pray for God to give you a renewed vision for the tasks He's called you to do.

4. Every Christian has a special calling from the Lord. We are all equal in Christ, and He has given women a special bond to support and encourage one another. Look at your relationships with other women. Have you been supportive of others? Are you the person others turn to when they are having a crisis? If not, commit to build strong relationships with others, knowing that God has a unique purpose for each of us.

QUESTIONS FOR GROUP DISCUSSION

1. In what ways would you like to change how you've been thinking about or doing homemaking?

2. How is God using your life in your home to minister to those around you? Is God showing you other opportunities He may want you to be involved in? What are they?

3. Share some creative ways you have found to spend time with the Lord in the midst of your busy family life.

5

SURVIVAL TRAINING FOR MARRIAGE

Who can find a virtuous wife? For her worth is far above rubies. The heart of her husband safely trusts her; so he will have no lack of gain. She does him good and not evil all the days of her life.

—Proverbs 31:10–12

H ave you ever heard the phrase, "There is no such thing as a perfect marriage"? Have you ever wondered if that phrase is really true or whether a perfect marriage is an impossibility? Since we're imperfect people, a perfect marriage would seem difficult to attain. Yet God had something special in mind when He created marriage between a husband and wife. He had an extraordinary purpose that could only be accomplished through the union of two people. Did that mean marriage would be easy? No! There are many things we need to understand when we approach the subject of marriage. Most importantly, we need to see marriage from God's perspective.

> *Love suffers long and is kind; love does not envy;*
> *love does not parade itself, is not puffed up;*
> *does not behave rudely, does not seek its own, is*
> *not provoked, thinks no evil; does not rejoice in*
> *iniquity, but rejoices in the truth; bears all*
> *things, believes all things, hopes all things,*
> *endures all things. Love never fails.*
> *—1 Corinthians 13:4–8*

CHANGING DREAMS

Before I was married, I had an idealistic picture of what my future husband would be like. Daydreaming led to delightful visions of a tall, dark, and handsome man who was always in a good mood and quick with a joke and a smile. He would have aspirations for neatness, always meticulously hanging up his jacket when he came home from work. And of course, he would always help around the house without being asked.

So many hopes and dreams were wrapped up in what I thought I wanted in a husband. Yet, as with my desire to be a missionary, I discovered that my idea of what would be "perfect" for me changed with maturity and experience. Things I thought were extremely important to me before I was married paled in comparison to what really was essential. A godly character became far more valuable to me than personal habits or personal appearances. Not only am I unconcerned that my husband has never hung up his jacket anywhere except the back of the dining-room chair after a long day, but whenever he does, it now brings a sense of peace because it means he's home.

Visions of being a successful and appreciated pastor's wife changed into a desire to faithfully serve alongside my husband through difficult situations. Dreaming of having a marriage without any disagreements or conflicts evolved into seeking a mature relationship that allowed us to talk through any situation, no matter how painful or difficult.

My hopes and prayers for my marriage today are completely different from those I had on my wedding day. My definition of *perfect* has also changed. No longer does it focus solely on my expectations and what I would like my husband to be; instead, it focuses on what we become together.

> *Therefore know that the LORD your God, He is*
> *God, the faithful God who keeps covenant and*
> *mercy for a thousand generations with those who*
> *love Him and keep His commandments.*
> —*Deuteronomy 7:9*

GOD'S PLAN FOR MARRIAGE

Marriage is so important, God used a special word in Scripture to help His people understand the significance of what He was doing: covenant (Malachi 2:14–15). The Israelites understood how important the covenant was to them. A covenant was a promise between God and His people that could not be broken without serious and dire consequences (Deuteronomy 11:26–28). It was a willing commitment the people made to the Lord, choosing Him as their God and deciding to follow His directions and commands. They had a responsibility to keep their side of the covenant, regardless of the situation, and to trust the Lord to honor His promises. In return, God pledged to bless them; to give them His presence, His wisdom, His guidance; and to lead them to victory over their enemies. Keeping this covenant was their life; it meant success, fulfillment, prosperity, and triumph (Deuteronomy 11:1–32).

In the New Testament, it is through Jesus' death and resurrection, the shedding of His own blood, which allows God's people to enter into a "new covenant" with Him, bringing salvation to all who choose to believe (Matthew 26:28).

The depth of love that God demonstrated in this covenant is the same profound compassion He brings to the marriage covenant. He wants our lives to be filled with the joy, success, and fulfillment that come through being one with another person in marriage. Because of this, God provides all of His resources to help us experience a successful relationship—the same resources He makes available in our Christian walk. He knows how challenging the task is, so He gives us access to His grace, mercy, forgiveness, patience, and love—everything we need to succeed in marriage.

> *"Have you not read that He who made them at the beginning 'made them male and female,' and said, 'For this reason a man shall leave his father and mother and be joined to his wife, and the two shall become one flesh'? So then, they are no longer two but one flesh. Therefore what God has joined together, let not man separate."*
> —*Matthew 19:4–6*

INDEPENDENCE VERSUS INTERDEPENDENCE

Although I married straight out of university, Henry had lived on his own for several years before we married. As a young man, he held a number of difficult jobs to pay his way through university. Growing up in northern British Columbia, Canada, he spent summers working hard as a deckhand on fishing boats, cleaning fish, surrounded by tough and hardened men. He lived in a military-type town near the Alaskan border and was privy to the sounds and smells of the bars and dance halls. His family even started a church in a local dance hall. They were given permission to use the facility for Sunday services as long as they cleaned up the mess from Saturday night's happy hour. Because of these encounters, Henry had a lot of experience with all types of people.

When we pastored our first church in San Pablo, California, Henry quickly became known as one who could deal with the troubled and discarded of society. Some of the local police would pick up small-time offenders and offer them a choice: spend some time in jail or go talk to the preacher. At all hours of the night, policemen would knock on our door and ask Henry, "Would you mind talking to this person?" From Hell's Angels members to local drunks, we saw people from all walks of life on our doorstep. In fact, Henry was even honored by local law enforcement for the dramatic effect our church had in reducing crime in the community.

One Friday night, a woman who had family members involved in our church asked Henry to perform a wedding for her daughter. Since we didn't know the woman or her daughter, Henry asked questions, assessing whether both parents were in agreement with the decision. All involved assured Henry that there was nothing keeping the young couple from marrying, so he performed the ceremony.

The next day, we got a call from a neighbor of the girl's family. The new bride's father had a gun and was going to kill the couple as well as his wife for helping them marry when he had been against it. They asked Henry, as the pastor, to please come and help. Henry rushed out the door, leaving me terrified and alone. What would this father do when the preacher who had married the couple tried to talk to him? Would he blame Henry? I agonized for hours, cleaning every cupboard and closet as I waited anxiously to hear a word from my husband—or the police.

Later that evening, Henry finally came home and told me how he had taken the gun out of the father's hand and spent the next several hours counseling the family. I couldn't believe it! He had defused the situation hours before and hadn't bothered to call and let me know that everything was okay. In fact, it didn't even occur to him that he needed to call. He was functioning the way he always had, trusting the Lord to protect him. But he hadn't realized that I would be upset and worried about him. He loved me, but he never thought about how this situation would affect me.

After I calmed down, we had a long talk about responsibility and compromise. I needed to trust my husband and his judgment in difficult situations, and he needed to include me in what was happening. I had to help him understand how I was feeling, and he in turn needed to adjust his actions and communicate more effectively with me.

By God's design, a married couple can no longer function as individuals; they must learn to function together as a unit. When we join together with someone in marriage, we give up our independence to become one with our spouses. Decisions we make must be based not merely on what we want or think we need but on what is best for the family. Every decision we make affects our spouses.

In marriage, God's intention is that we will never have to make an important decision alone, nor will we have to face difficult situations by ourselves. When a crisis arises, we will have someone to lean on, and when times of joy occur, we will have someone to celebrate with. If we have children, we will work together with our spouses through the ups and downs of teaching our children the ways of the Lord. We will grow and mature together, learning more about the Lord and each other as the years go by. Sharing our lives and experiencing the depth of a mature relationship that comes through time are only small aspects of God's magnificent plan for marriage.

A merry heart does good, like medicine,
but a broken spirit dries the bones.
—Proverbs 17:22

LAUGHTER IS GOOD MEDICINE

A few months after we moved to Saskatoon, we had a terrifying experience that could have had a lasting negative impact on our first year there. In the middle of the night, I was heading toward the bathroom. Since we still didn't have curtains on the windows yet, it was easy for me to look into our children's rooms to make sure they were sleeping. While checking our two youngest sons, my eyes focused on a dark shape crouching by their bunk bed. There was an intruder in the house!

When he realized I saw him, the intruder started to advance toward me, and I shouted, "Henry, there's a stranger in the house!"

"You're just imagining things," he replied.

"No, he's coming, and he's going to hit me!"

Thump! Henry's feet hit the floor. The robber pushed past me and ran out the back door into the alley. Henry ran out the same door and out into the front yard, waving his arms and yelling. But

EMMA REVELL MOODY
(1842–1903)

Emma Moody was born in London but moved to Chicago in 1849. She loved knowledge and became a Sunday-school teacher at 15 and a school teacher at 17.

Affectionately known as "Mrs. D. L.," Emma was married to one of the great revival speakers of that time: Dwight L. Moody.[1] But what was exceptional about Emma was how she saw her marriage. She sought to do all she could to make life easier for her husband, who traveled extensively and was very passionate about his work. Moody's son said of his parents "In thirty-seven years of their married life she was the only one who had never tried to hold him back from anything he wanted to do and was always in sympathy with any new venture. She was his 'balance wheel'."[2]

Emma sought to make a home away from home, since she and her husband constantly traveled in England and America. She took care of the finances and correspondence and sought to do all she could to free her husband to follow God's will for his life. She did these things without seeking praise for herself but always tried to help her husband look good.[3]

"Aunt Emma and Uncle Dwight were so perfectly one that nobody could possibly tell which was the one," said one of their nieces.[4]

the intruder was long gone. After calling the police and making a quick search through the house, the only thing we found missing was my purse. We were told that the previous tenant owned a business and was known to keep the weekly payroll with him at the house, providing a nice, easy target.

We could have been terribly shaken by this experience because we were new to the area and just getting settled. Instead, since no one was hurt we began to laugh! Little did our home invader know that we had next to nothing, so there wasn't anything to steal. In fact, when the boys found my purse in the alley later that morning, they discovered a $10 bill in the bottom that I knew wasn't mine, since I rarely had cash of any kind. We all chuckled, thinking that the robber must have felt sorry for us and left the money, assuming that we were harder up than he was. Henry deserved points for having the courage to give chase, but for years now, we've laughed about him running down the street after the bandit in his Fruit of the Looms!

Our house has always been known as a home of laughter. Our children would comment (and complain) that they could hear us laughing from several houses away. Laughing at ourselves and looking for the lighter side of situations has brought us a great deal of joy over the years.

Whenever people ask me for marriage advice, I always tell them to look for the humorous side of things. Never go to bed unless you've laughed about three situations that happened during the day. It may take a while to think of something funny, but when Henry and I talked in the evenings, no matter how difficult our day was, we would laugh together. It helped us in several ways: It changed our perspective on the situation, it solidified our resolve to face things together, it relieved our stress, it kept our focus off ourselves, and it was much more fun than crying!

> *"If anyone comes to Me and does not hate his father*
> *and mother, wife and children, brothers and sisters,*
> *yes, and his own life also, he cannot be My disciple."*
> — *Luke 14:26*

THE KEY

No one would claim that marriage is uncomplicated or trouble-free any more than one would suggest that the Christian walk is effortless. But God never intended for us to muddle through the difficulties in our own strength (Matthew 11:29). He wants to walk with us every step of the way. He has covenanted with us to provide what we need to succeed (Matthew 7:7, 2 Peter 1:3–8). He has promised us all the wisdom, patience, love, endurance, and strength that we need for every day if we follow and obey Him. Trusting God and seeking His guidance—not just as individuals but together as a couple—is the key to a successful marriage.

Many people ask how Henry and I ever found time to spend together as a couple with five children and a booming ministry that constantly kept Henry busy. The answer: We chose to take the time and make it a priority. Every evening, usually after ten o'clock when the kids were asleep and Henry had returned from teaching a Bible study, he and I would have a pot of tea and a plate of cookies and talk about all that God had done throughout the day. We would share our struggles, pray for our children, and spend time fellowshipping together. It wasn't a time to criticize or address each other's shortcomings. The time was so special to us. The most amazing thing was that we often found we were learning the same things, just in different ways. God taught us separately about our relationship with Him, which always led to greater strength in our marriage. And it built a trust that has never been broken.

To this day, Henry and I talk together every day—or we talk on the phone if we're not in the same location. Now, instead of talking and praying in the evening, we fellowship over coffee in the mornings. We chose to establish this time early in our marriage, regardless of how hectic our lives were. The communication and fellowship we have shared all these years have been the foundation of our marriage. When trouble came, we could always talk and openly share our struggles without fear. We sought to never be judgmental, but to listen, support, and encourage each other. Even in difficult times, we could still turn toward each other and talk through our challenges. Without that communication and fellowship, our marriage would have been empty.

> *Charm is deceitful and beauty is passing, but a woman who fears the LORD, she shall be praised.*
> —*Proverbs 31:30*

WHEN TROUBLE COMES

While living in Saskatoon, I reached a point where I became overwhelmed. I was raising five little kids under the age of 10, and I was beginning to feel completely weighed down. I felt alone and in desperate need of help, a vacation—anything! My husband was often gone, starting new work in unreached areas. I had no money to go out for coffee or treat myself. My parents, at the time, were serving as missionaries in Africa, and my sister and her family lived in Europe, also working as missionaries. I was struggling without my usual support from family or close friends. I felt as though I was drowning.

After cleaning the house one day, I decided to take all the kids outside for a walk. For once, I wasn't paying attention to the children or where we were going. Instead, I was pouring my heart out to the Lord. I told Him that I didn't think I could handle everything on my own. In reality, I wanted some sympathy and thought that God should tell my husband to help me more at home. I'm sure that would have been the advice from my friends or family. But, not surprisingly, God had a different answer and solution for me. He told me, "Henry is doing exactly what I have asked Him to do. I will help you raise your children."

With this answer, I had a decision to make: I could force my husband to stay home more regularly and help with the children, or I could trust the Lord with my situation and my family. I chose to have faith in the Lord and believe that my husband was doing what God told him to do.

There were times when our children needed their father to be home. During those times, it was easier for Henry to stay because he knew I wouldn't have asked unless it was absolutely necessary. This was an important lesson for me. Yes, life continued to be difficult. But I knew my husband was earnestly seeking God's will. He wasn't simply working himself to death or wasting time; he was being obedient to our Lord.

This realization made a big impact on our marriage. I didn't have to resent what God called my husband to do. I could help him be successful. I didn't have to arrange my husband's schedule based on what I needed. Instead, I trusted him to obey the Lord. I also found that I didn't have to do everything in my own strength anymore, because God promised to help me. Instead of turning to my husband all the time for wisdom, I could turn to the Lord for guidance.

I became more confident in what God called Henry to do, knowing and trusting that I could handle the home front. Henry could also have confidence in my relationship with the Lord and believe that I would seek the Lord's wisdom when dealing with any situation. Often, the Lord would give me strength when I had exhausted my own. And He regularly protected my children when I couldn't keep them from harm myself.

Being away from home was difficult for my husband because he wanted to be with his family. But as a young boy, he had made a promise to the Lord that he would go wherever God invited him to go. My strength in the Lord helped Henry fulfill that promise.

Many years later at a conference in Texas, the leader asked me to stand and tell everyone where our children were and what they were doing. I mentioned that the older three boys were in seminary in Texas, one boy was finishing university at Hardin-Simmons, and our daughter was starting university in Oklahoma. All the children were doing well and seeking to obey the Lord. After sharing I sat down. Immediately I felt God saying, "See? I was faithful to my promise to you."

God honored our obedience to Him. He helped me through those early days. He kept His hand on each one of our children, eventually calling them into different kinds of Christian service. And He gave each of them a godly spouse to partner with them as they served the Lord together.

How would things be different if I had insisted that my husband stay home regularly instead of starting mission churches? I don't know. Maybe I wouldn't have trusted the Lord or grown in my relationship with Him as I needed to. Perhaps I would have even stifled my husband's relationship with the Lord, because he would have considered himself disobedient to his vow to the Lord. But I know that I, once again, experienced the promise of the Lord in my life, in my family, and in my marriage. God helped me see that when He was central in my life, I would have all I needed to enjoy a successful marriage. I would be able to love my husband unselfishly and help him obey all that God had for him.

Make vows to the LORD your God, and pay them.
— Psalm 76:11

My husband also sought to help me obey the Lord and keep my vows to Him. Henry knew that at several points in my Christian walk, I had made vows and commitments to the Lord. It was crucial to Henry that he not cause me to break my word to the Lord, and he sought to help me obey all that I knew God had called

PRISCILLA

Greet Priscilla and Aquila, my fellow workers in
Christ Jesus, who risked their own necks for my life,
to whom not only I give thanks, but also all the
churches of the Gentiles (Romans 16:3–4).

The apostle Paul saw Priscilla and her husband, Aquila, as a
model couple. They openly welcomed him into their home. They
were strong believers who had left their home in Italy because
of the persecution of the Jews from Rome. While in Corinth,
they made such an impression on Paul that they traveled to
Syria with him.

It was while Priscilla and Aquila were in Alexandria that
they were able to help guide the fiery speaker Apollos, who
was mighty in the Scriptures but needed discipling in His relationship with the Lord.

Although few places in Scripture mention this couple who
worked so closely together, there is enough to see what impact
they made. They began a church-planting movement that was
modeled in their home. They were bold in their witness and had
a love for their fellow believers. They were well known to the
other Christians, especially to Paul, who frequently sent them
greetings. And they were an example to all who knew them of
how a couple could work together, both in the workplace and in
serving the Lord. (See Acts 18:2–3, 18–19, 24–26; Romans
16:3–4; 1 Corinthians 16:19; 2 Timothy 4:19.)

me to do. Before Henry and I were married, we talked through all the commitments I had made to the Lord. My husband wrote them down, and to this day, he seeks to help me be faithful to those vows. Even though we were joined in marriage and were made one, it didn't negate the promises I had made to God earlier in my life. I would be called to account for my commitments, as would Henry. Vows are serious to the Lord and should never be taken lightly or forgotten.

> *Yet she is your companion*
> *and your wife by covenant.*
> —*Malachi 2:14*

COMMUNICATION LEADS TO FELLOWSHIP

One day I was talking to a woman I met at the airport in Atlanta. We were both waiting in Delta's Crown Room for our flights, and we started to have a friendly conversation. She was in the country visiting her children, but traveling alone. I discovered that she had lost her husband 15 years earlier. She revealed that although she deeply loved her children, they could never take the place of the fellowship she had experienced with her husband. Nothing could restore the hole in her life that was left when her husband died. In fact, she told me that she missed him as much at that moment in her life as she ever had. They had had a beautiful marriage that had been filled with companionship and years of spending time with each other. The communication they had, even without needing to say anything, could never be replaced. This type of relationship comes through taking the time to get to know each other. It takes work, patience, and honesty, but having a strong marriage is worth it!

COMMUNICATION AND OUR FIRST CHRISTMAS

Learning to communicate comes through experience. At the beginning of our marriage, it was challenging to find the balance between the desire to be positive, supportive, and strong and wanting my husband to understand my point of view and value my feelings above the concerns of others.

I was so excited about my first Christmas as a wife. My mother had taught me well, and I knew how to make a good meal with all the trimmings. I was up early that morning, cooking the turkey and preparing several dishes: the made-from-scratch dressing, home-made rolls, sweet potatoes, green-bean casserole, and an assortment of salads. I had bought the most beautiful 20-pound turkey I could find and cooked it to perfection. I also set the table with our new china and crystal. One might assume that we were expecting half the church to join us for dinner, but I had prepared all this for just the two of us.

I tried to make the day as special as I could. However, as often happens in the home of a pastor, just as I had placed the last dish of food on the table and we had taken our seats, there was a knock on the door. A young couple who had lost a child the day before was having a difficult time, and their aunt had come to seek Henry's help. Could he go and comfort them? Henry immediately left with the aunt and tried to help the family. Being the caring, supportive young wife I was, I didn't say anything to dissuade him.

On the outside, I was okay, but on the inside, I was crushed that he would leave me to eat Christmas dinner alone. Henry didn't return until late that evening. Since I was young and disheartened, instead of giving the food to someone or seeing if there were any needs we could meet, I just cleaned up and threw most of it away. We were leaving early the next day on a trip, and our refrigerator was so small, it barely held the turkey. Henry didn't even get to taste the food.

We both learned some valuable lessons that day. This family's situation was tragic, and although they weren't alone, they wanted advice and comfort from their pastor. Henry learned that it would have been okay to say, "I've just sat down for dinner with my wife. Let me eat something, and I'll be there in half an hour." A few minutes wouldn't have made a tremendous difference to the couple, who didn't realize we were eating. But it would have mattered to me. Five or ten minutes of talking through a plan for our time together, setting a time to call and let me know what was going on or when he would be home, words of appreciation for my efforts— all of these things would have greatly encouraged me that Christmas morning and would have let me know that I was as important to my husband as those people who were hurting that day.

It's vital to treasure your spouse and all that is significant to him. Yes, God did call Henry to be a pastor, but He also gave him the responsibility of being my husband. Our home and marriage are important. I learned that I needed to communicate my desires to my husband. If I had waited for him to pick up my subtle hints, I would still be waiting! I want him to understand my heart, what I am thinking and feeling, so he can know me better. It makes our relationship stronger.

We spent a lot of time talking through this situation and both came to a better understanding of what we were thinking and feeling. Consequently, this incident was never repeated.

Learning to communicate in a marriage takes a lot of honesty and listening, but with practice, it gets easier every time. I also learned not to fix a 20-pound turkey for two people, and since that time, I've always tried to invite those who don't have any family nearby to celebrate the holidays with us.

> *Husbands, likewise, dwell with them with*
> *understanding, giving honor to the wife, as to the*
> *weaker vessel, and as being heirs together of the*
> *grace of life, that your prayers may not be hindered.*
> *— 1 Peter 3:7*

WHEN HOPE IS DISTANT

When we were serving in San Pablo, one of my friends was in a difficult and explosive marriage. We often worked together in the children's nursery at church, and I knew she was suffering. During an argument one day, she taunted her husband about the true parentage of her second child. She soon realized the enormous mistake she had made in her anger, but she didn't yet fully understand the consequences. Her husband took her rash words to heart. He became unbearable, withholding basic needs from the new baby and not giving his wife money to buy clothing or toys for the child. She was desperate, often borrowing my baby lotions and diaper-rash cream while we were at church together. I was happy to help her and was extremely concerned about her situation.

One morning she called me, furious and seriously contemplating ways to kill her husband. I asked what she needed me to do to help her. She asked for enough money to catch a bus to her parents' home for herself and her two children, and she pleaded with me to drive her to the station. I didn't have any money, but I made a few calls and found a kind church member who would give her the money. My husband came home and took care of our children while I picked up the woman and her sweet children and took them to the bus terminal. To avoid a possible tragedy, there was nothing I wouldn't do to help her get away and take the time she needed to gain some perspective in a safe environment. When her husband found out I had taken her to the station, he called Henry, who then spent several hours trying to help him calm down and think through the situation.

We moved to Southern California not long after this. To my utter surprise, a few years later, she and her husband and children showed up at our church. They looked us up and drove five hundred miles to thank us for helping them through a dangerous crisis in their marriage. They both needed the time apart—she desperately needed intervention, and he used the time to think through his anger and turn it over to the Lord.

Now they were standing in front of us with a third child in their arms. My friend beamed at me, and it was clear that they were happily married and seeking to follow the Lord. I was so thankful that she was able to trust me when she was in need and that I was able to help her.

When two Christians marry, entering into a covenant together with God as their witness, God will unfold wonderful things in their marriage. Although difficult times will inevitably come, every marriage that is firmly grounded in the Lord can withstand any storm. God's love, mercy, grace, and forgiveness are enough to overcome any situation in our lives and to carry us through our journey in marriage.

When the foundation of a marriage isn't based on a commitment to the Lord, however, it can be difficult or seemingly impossible to find a way through life's troubles. It will be challenging to have the full and meaningful marriage God intended if you are married to someone who doesn't trust the Lord to guide him. Yet God's promise to every believer remains the same, regardless of the spiritual state of our spouses: "Trust in the LORD with all your heart, and lean not on your own understanding; In all of your ways acknowledge Him, and He shall direct your paths" (Proverbs 3:5–6).

A Christian always has access to all the promises of God. Regardless of the situation, God is always with us, wanting to help us in our lives and marriages. Our mistakes or failures don't cancel the love of God or His ability to give us peace and joy. Some circumstances are difficult to handle, but God's wisdom and guidance will always be available to His people when they seek Him.

"Therefore you shall be perfect, just
as your Father in heaven is perfect."
—*Matthew 5:48*

........⚜️........

There is such a thing as a perfect marriage, but not in the sense of our youthful imaginations. No one is free from mistakes. When two people, who have experienced the love and mercy of Christ, apply the same compassion and forgiveness in their marriage, it can be perfect—as perfect as God intended. Each day is a clean slate, free from disagreements or hurt feelings of yesterday if communication and forgiveness are demonstrated. As Christ has forgiven us, we should also forgive each other (Colossians 3:13). That includes our spouses! Just as a Christian will inevitably make mistakes, seek forgiveness, and return to a right relationship with the Lord, mistakes within a marriage can make it stronger instead of tearing it apart. Allowing God to direct us and doing everything He has commanded us to do—communicating with our spouses, putting them first above all others, having trust and openness in the home—will lead to a lasting and fulfilled marriage.

Regardless of our marriage situations, nothing can thwart God's love for us. There are times when we need help, times when we need to turn to those God brings into our lives. As Christians, God doesn't leave us alone in times of trouble but provides the wisdom and strength to follow Him. Sometimes our choices come with a price, regardless of whether a choice was made in ignorance or out of disobedience. But nothing can keep us from experiencing the love of God in our lives when we seek Him.

QUESTIONS FOR DEEPER REFLECTION

1. When you were married, God was a witness to your vows. He witnessed your covenant together and committed to help you become all He intended you to be when He brought you and your spouse together. Think back to your wedding and all the love you had that day. How have things changed since then? Has your love deepened and matured, making your original feelings pale in comparison? Has your commitment to "forever" slipped, or is it as strong as ever? Think through your vows and renew them in your heart, asking God to help you grow and mature in your relationship with your spouse.

2. Communication in any marriage takes commitment, work, forgiveness, and an endless supply of patience. If your lives are becoming too crowded with other activities or responsibilities, talk to your husband about setting apart some time— at least once a week—to talk or just be together. When you get together, seek to understand what God is doing in your husband's life. Even if he isn't a Christian, God will be working around him!

3. Without forgiveness, a marriage is destined to be painful and filled with problems. Scripture tells us that we will be forgiven in the same way we forgive others who have wronged us (Matthew 6:12). This doesn't mean that if you're being abused, you constantly forgive your spouse and fail to seek help when it's needed. But holding anger or bitterness in your heart will hurt you, your marriage, your family, and your relationship with the Lord. Search your heart to see if you are

holding something against your husband. If so, confess it to the Lord and ask Him to restore your heart and your relationship with your husband.

4. Do you think you have a perfect marriage? If your definition of *perfect* means never making mistakes, you won't see perfection in anything life has to offer. But if you and your husband daily seek to follow the Lord, communicate with each other, treasure each other, and forgive one another you'll have everything God intended you to have in your marriage. Don't settle for just a good marriage when you can have God's best!

QUESTIONS FOR GROUP DISCUSSION

1. Discuss the idea of a perfect marriage. Has your understanding of what a marriage can be changed? If so, how?
2. Communication is important in any relationship, but especially in a marriage. What ways have you found to facilitate better communication? What changes do you need to make in the way you relate to your spouse?
3. Discuss ways that each of you has found to set aside time to be together with your husband.

6

THE NECESSITY OF PRAYER

Rejoice always, pray without ceasing, in everything give thanks; for this is the will of God in Christ Jesus for you.
—*1 Thessalonians 5:16–18*

As a pastor, my husband often led Bible studies or traveled during the weekdays. One evening, he was free to stay at home, and I thought it would be a good opportunity for him to spend some time with the kids and say their bedtime prayers with them. He was pleased to do so and enjoyed hearing the kids pray. Later that evening, I heard a little voice whispering, "Mom, Mom, Mom . . ." from our daughter's room.

When I went to check on her, she motioned me closer and asked, "Mom, can you pray with me?"

I was surprised at her request, because I knew that Henry had prayed with her before she went to bed.

"Didn't your father pray with you?" I asked.

She nodded her head. "Yes, but Dad doesn't know how to pray right."

I turned red-faced, choked back the laughter, knelt down, and prayed with my daughter. I teased my very spiritual husband about this for a long time. What our daughter was really saying was that her dad didn't follow our normal bedtime routine in prayer.

"If you abide in Me, and My words abide in you, you will ask what you desire, and it shall be done for you."

—John 15:7

THE IMPORTANCE OF SCRIPTURE
IN PRAYER

This same daughter, several years later, would face her own crisis, and the strength of her prayer life would be paramount. When Carrie was 16, she underwent a terrible regimen of chemotherapy to fight cancer that was growing in her chest cavity. We had an excellent cancer clinic in Vancouver, but treatment in the 1980s wasn't as advanced as it is today.

One Sunday morning during the Sunday-school hour, the small group of youth from our church was praying. Carrie was also praying because she had an important meeting with the doctors the next day to determine how the cancer was responding to the treatment and how many more months of chemotherapy were needed. It was a scary prospect for a teenager. In the middle of her prayer time, she felt led to Psalm 103. She had been reading through the Psalms, and on that day, the Holy Spirit drew her to that passage. As she was praying that God would work a miracle in her life (as many others were), she read the first verses of this psalm:

Bless the LORD, O my soul;
    and all that is within me,
bless His holy name!
Bless the LORD, O my soul,
    and forget not all His benefits:
Who forgives all your iniquities,
    who heals all your diseases (verses 1–3).

Although she had read these verses before, she believed that the Lord gave her this passage as a direct answer to prayer. Her God had not only saved and cleansed her soul, but He had also healed her body. She told her youth teacher what God had revealed to her, and she underwent the multitude of tests the next day with a light heart.

It came as no surprise to her when the doctors amazingly found the cancer in remission. They had been testing to see if she needed an additional three to six months of chemotherapy, but instead the doctors ended her chemo treatments and started radiation treatments to make sure the cancer wouldn't return. Carrie's ordeal wasn't over, but the disease was gone.

During our daughter's illness, God gave Henry this scripture: "This sickness is not unto death, but for the glory of God, that the Son of God may be glorified through it" (John 11:4). God often answers our prayers through Scripture. Andrew Murray once said,

> When you pray, you must seek to know God correctly. It is
> through the Word that the Holy Spirit gives you right thoughts
> of Him. The Word will also teach you how wretched and
> sinful you are. It reveals to you all the wonders that God will
> do for you and the strength He will give you to do His will.
> The Word teaches you how to pray with strong desire, with
> firm faith, and with constant perseverance. The Word teaches
> you not only what you are, but also what you may become
> through God's grace. Above all, it reminds you each day that
> Christ is the great Intercessor and allows you to pray in His
> name.[1]

Reading and learning the Bible go hand in hand with prayer. The more you understand about the Lord through reading the Scriptures, the more you can experience of Him in prayer. The Holy Spirit uses Scripture in our lives to instruct and guide, often bringing special verses to mind in times of difficulty or as an answer to prayer. If we aren't familiar with Scripture or we neglect time in God's Word, our prayer life will never achieve the fullness God intended it to have.

> *At the beginning of your supplications the*
> *command went out, and I have come to*
> *tell you, for you are greatly beloved.*
> *—Daniel 9:23*

SURPRISES IN PRAYER

I think the Lord must have a wonderful sense of humor. Just as I had my dreams of the person I would someday marry, Henry did as well and had been praying about his spouse for many years. At the top of his list was a healthy wife who would be able to serve at his side, a woman who would provide company in his many travels and have an equal partnership in the marriage.

On our first day of marriage, Henry thought that God had chosen *not* to answer His prayers in a positive way. Not only didn't I help with the driving (mainly because I had forgotten my purse with my driver's license), but I slept the entire way to our honeymoon spot. And the next day while washing dishes, I passed out and dumped water all over myself and the floor!

Poor Henry thought he had married a low-energy, sickly woman. After one day, all his worst fears were being realized. I was upset because I thought Henry had thrown water on me to wake me up, not knowing I had spilled it myself when I fell. What Henry didn't know was that I had been so excited about the wedding, I hadn't slept in about two weeks—not to mention that my stomach had so many butterflies I wasn't able to eat properly. I was literally worn out from all the events and lack of sleep leading up to the wedding.

Often, what looks like a negative answer from the Lord can actually be the very response we've been praying for. It took Henry awhile to realize that God had indeed answered his prayers and had given him a healthy partner who enjoyed hard work. Sometimes it's difficult to see immediate results when we pray. It is possible that God has already granted our request, but, like Henry, we may not know it at the time.

> *Likewise the Spirit also helps in our weaknesses.*
> *For we do not know what we should pray for as we*
> *ought, but the Spirit Himself makes intercession for*
> *us with groanings which cannot be uttered.*
> —*Romans 8:26*

THE POWER OF PRAYER

The winters in Saskatoon were bitterly cold, long, and dark, and the roads were notoriously treacherous. There city usually kept the local roads well maintained with salt and gravel, but the outlying roads weren't so well cared for. Regardless, I was rarely concerned about my children driving. They were all experienced drivers, knowing the dangers of winter driving and how to handle a vehicle on ice and snow. We always prayed for their safety, but I don't remember a time when I was fearful for them. But for some reason, this time was different.

My three oldest sons had to attend a weekend student conference in Calgary. They had no option not to go because one son was the student president for Canada, and one was the local campus president. Several other representatives from the universities in our area were also going to the conference with our sons.

The weather was bitterly cold that weekend, and the road conditions weren't the best. I was deeply unsettled and told the boys to make sure they didn't all ride in the same car, because we had recently read about an entire family that was killed in a single-car accident. My sons agreed, of course, humoring me while chuckling, then they asked me which son I wanted in the car that was going to be in the accident. I wasn't as amused as they were!

That Sunday, I was washing dishes alone and was using the quiet to talk to the Lord. My concern for my children never lessened. Suddenly, I was gripped with an overwhelming sense that I needed to pray specifically for the boys' safety. I ran into the bedroom and shook Henry out of his afternoon nap. We immediately got on our knees together and prayed for the safety and welfare of those on the trip.

Later that evening, we heard the boys come in the back door. "What happened at three o'clock today?" I asked. They gave me a funny look and started to tell the story about what happened on their trip. They were driving home when one of the cars hit some black ice and spun out of control. It started to careen into oncoming traffic, right in front of an 18-wheel truck. The boy who was driving had no control over the car. In front of them was the truck, and on the other side was a half-frozen pond. At the last second, the car swerved to the other side of the road and came to a stop. Two of my three boys were in this car. When we looked at the time frame, it came as no surprise that it happened in the moments when my husband and I were praying for their safety.

I have no way of knowing what was on God's heart when He chose to alert me to these events. He may have wanted our family to see His power in a real and practical way. Perhaps He wanted us to experience a deeper understanding of the importance of prayer in our lives so we would have the prayer life necessary for pioneer missions.

My children were in the Lord's hands, and He didn't need my help to save them. In His divine grace, however, He chose to sensitize me to the danger they were in and caused us to pray at the very moment our children were in trouble. He gave our family a glimpse of His divine power and His absolute sovereignty in our lives. Henry and I would have been thankful to the Lord for protecting our children without His including us, but through His mercy, we were able to feel a part of His saving power.

It's still astounding to me that God chooses to work through His people, accomplishing what He alone can do. Why He seeks a relationship with us and chooses to work through us will always be a great mystery. Yet we know this is how He has always related to people. God could have built His chosen people from the dust if He had wanted to and established them as a nation; instead He chose to work through the life of Abraham (Genesis 12:1–3). Did God really need Moses to lead the children of Israel out of slavery in Egypt (Exodus 3–14), or could He have accomplished it by sending an angel? Did Gideon need three hundred men to defeat the vast army of the Midianites for God to be successful (Judges 6–7)? Could God have utterly blasted Elijah's altar with fire (1 Kings 18:20–40), proving His lordship over all idols for the multitudes to see, without Elijah asking Him to do it? Did God need the small group of believers

HANNAH

And Hannah prayed and said: "My heart rejoices in the LORD; my horn is exalted in the LORD. I smile at my enemies, because I rejoice in Your salvation" (1 Samuel 2:1).

Hannah was living in a very difficult situation. Although her husband, Elkanah, deeply loved her, she was childless. Her husband also had another wife, a common arrangement for that day, and she was a constant source of antagonism and provocation for Hannah.

Elkanah deeply respected the Lord and "went up from his city yearly to worship and sacrifice to the Lord of hosts" (1 Samuel 1:3). Although Hannah wasn't required to go with him to worship the Lord, she did anyway.

During one of their yearly trips, Hannah poured her soul

praying in an upper room before He would release the Holy Spirit (Acts 2:1–4)? Could God have revealed His love and salvation message, saving thousands in one day and beginning the first church, without Peter's sermon (Acts 2:14–47)?

God can do anything He wants, and He isn't dependent on anyone else to accomplish His will. Yet He chooses to involve people in His work. We don't know the time and place God will come to us, alert us to His activity, and work through our lives. Therefore, it's up to us to always be ready, watching and praying. Keeping our lives so prepared before the Lord that we can discern His slightest whisper ought to be every believer's goal. Not paying

out to the Lord. Deeply distressed over how she had been treated by members of her family, she cried out in anguish to the One who had the power to change her situation. She made a vow that if God would give her a baby boy, she would give him back to the Lord for the rest of his life.

God heard Hannah and answered her cry by giving her a son. In return, Hannah kept her vow to her Lord and sent her son to live in the temple after he was weaned. What followed her obedience is a beautiful prayer that God chose to include in the Scriptures: 1 Samuel 2:1–10. God knew Hannah's heart; He knew that she loved Him and would keep her promise. Because of this, God honored Hannah and her obedience by allowing her son, Samuel, to become one of the greatest prophets recorded in Scripture.

attention to His voice doesn't necessarily mean He won't work, but it does mean that we won't experience God's power being released through our lives.

> *"So I sought for a man among them who would make a wall, and stand in the gap before Me on behalf of the land, that I should not destroy it; but I found no one."*
> —*Ezekiel 22:30*

TIMING IS EVERYTHING

Praying the moment God alerts you to a situation is essential. We don't have to wait until we're in a prayer closet or in a quiet place before we pray. There should be urgency in our praying, especially if the Holy Spirit alerts us to do it. Often, we won't be able to see all the results of our prayers or how God will use them to further His purposes. Our job is to be ready, listening, and obedient in prayer.

Carrie has a friend and colleague who recently endured a terrifying 11-hour kidnapping at gunpoint in Peru, along with two other workers. Two kidnappers left, stealing their vehicle, and the last one led the captives into the woods. It was a harrowing experience for the three people involved. Throughout the ordeal, Carrie's friend was praying that God would alert others of their need for prayer. For an unknown and miraculous reason, the remaining gunman left them to fend for themselves and find their way back to civilization, where they could find help. Many prayers were voiced to the Lord that day, and He chose to work in a mighty way on behalf of these missionaries.

When God reveals something to us while we're praying, it's always for a reason. Often, we won't understand all He is doing at the time, but at a later point, God may show us the results of our prayers. This was brought home to me in a very tangible way during a trip far from home.

My mother had been ill for some time, but since her condition was stable, I continued with my plans to travel with Henry. We traveled through Brazil, speaking at several different conferences and trying to encourage God's people.

> *Whatever the situation is, when God brings someone to mind or heightens your awareness for some reason, the time to pray is right then.*

Admittedly, my Portuguese is limited. In fact, the extent of it is about three sentences: "How are you?" "Can I have some coffee?" and "Where is the bathroom?" Knowing this, the leaders of the conferences were helpful, and we usually had translators with us.

During the middle of a conference, I received a message that my mother had been readmitted to the hospital. It was difficult to get a phone line out to call my father for more information. For some reason, the operator wasn't responding to my Portuguese—or even to my clearly spoken English! So I did the only thing I knew to do in this situation: I prayed! From this point on, the only information I would be given about my mother would come from the Lord.

I spent a great deal of time in prayer that afternoon while Henry was speaking at the conference. I had to trust that God would let me know what I needed to do and that He would respond to me in a timely manner. I really felt God leading me to cancel the rest of my trip, return to the States, and visit my mother. Although leaving early was expensive and difficult, my husband was supportive and encouraged me to follow what I felt God had told me to do.

When I arrived, my father was surprised to see me, knowing that I had planned to be out of the country for a few more days. He didn't understand why I had rearranged my schedule, because he felt that my mother's condition was no longer critical. The crisis I was contacted about had passed. In fact, he had informed my siblings that an immediate return wasn't necessary; it wasn't imperative to visit at that point.

By the time I arrived, my mother was doing better than she had in a long time. We were able to have several wonderful conversations. She reminded me of when I was critically ill during my childhood and how she cared for me. She reminisced about God's words to her and how He had great plans for me. At one point, my mother called me to her and said, "Marilynn, I love you!" It was such a blessing! I left briefly to get something to eat, and when I returned to her room, I was shocked to find that she had passed on to be with the Lord. Her last words to me were a reminder of her love.

The timing of God's answer to my prayer was perfect. There hadn't been a moment to spare. Although it looked as if my mother was getting better, God knew the future and how much time she really had. He knew how important my mother was to me and how crucial it was for me to talk to her one last time. He also knew how

BERTHA SMITH
(1888–1988)

If there is one thing that categorized Miss Bertha's life, it was a deep commitment to prayer. Through her many years on the mission field, both in China and Taiwan, her prayers led to sweeping revival and countless people coming to the saving knowledge of Christ.

As a child, Bertha was very bright and always strove to be the best. Yet she struggled for years under the weight of her sin and pride and joked, "If the Lord could ever save anyone the wrong way, He would have saved me," after all her struggles to find Him.[2]

When she did come to Christ, it wasn't long before she was led to serve in China with the Southern Baptists. She was appointed in 1917.[3] Her story for the next 41 years on the mission field is of the love she had for the Lord and her deep commitment to trust and obey Him at all costs. She saw God's protection through both World War II and the Communist takeover of China.

Before God brought about the sweeping revivals in the Shantung Province, Bertha came to understand that one life not yielded completely to the Lord would keep away God's blessing. After the missionaries were pure before the Lord, the blessing came, starting with God's people, His church, and then spreading across China.[4] Bertha believed that if God's people didn't pray, there would never be a revival. Her prayer life made a difference and forever impacted God's kingdom.

important my mother's affirmation and love for me were, and He didn't want me to miss it. Trusting God's words to me, leaving in the middle of very important work to return to the United States, and my futile attempts to get a phone line out of the country—all of this led to one of my life's most beautiful memories. I would have trusted the words of my father if I had been able to get in touch with him. Instead, I listened only to the words of my heavenly Father, who held the future in His hands.

> *"Again I say to you that if two of you agree on*
> *earth concerning anything that they ask,*
> *it will be done for them by My Father in heaven.*
> *For where two or three are gathered together in*
> *My name, I am there in the midst of them."*
> —*Matthew 10:19–20*

PERSEVERANCE IN PRAYER

When we moved to Vancouver in 1982, Henry became the director of missions for the association of churches in that area. Initially, we joined a larger church to give the children some stability. Meanwhile, Henry preached in other churches that needed help or were without a pastor.

It wasn't too surprising that I was asked to teach a women's Sunday-school class in the church we had joined, and I was delighted to help out. That feeling lasted until I heard about the controversy regarding my "taking over" the women's adult Sunday-school class. The director of the Sunday-school program thought the women's adult class was getting too big and wanted to split the group in half. The problem was that he wasn't really giving the women a say in which class they would attend. Well, I wasn't going to be a part of that! Instead, I offered to teach a class for those who weren't already involved in Sunday school, allowing God to bring to us the women He wanted to attend. There was much relief for those who didn't want to leave their favorite teacher and all their friends, as well as for the Sunday-school director, who was about to be lynched!

God began to bring hurting and broken women to my class. Women from all walks of life came—from deacon's wives to those who had never been involved in the mainstream life of the church. I discovered that they all had a common problem: a struggling child. Some had children who were Christians but weren't obeying the Lord. Others were suffering because they knew their children weren't believers in Christ and were heading for serious, life-changing mistakes.

Our little class became a safe haven for women to share honestly, often for the first time, the pain they were experiencing over their children. We shared together, cried together, and prayed together for our children. When one mother had a difficult and painful week with her child, another had an encouraging week, and together we encouraged one another. After I left the class to help Henry in another church, the women continued meeting, even deciding to meet on Fridays to pray for their children. Slowly, God answered the prayers to reclaim their children for His name's sake.

It was hard to leave when God called us to serve in Atlanta, but I remained in close contact with that group. One year after we moved to Atlanta, I was given the opportunity to go back and visit the church. I talked with the ladies who were in that class to see how they were doing with their children. To my delight, every child we had prayed for was now following the Lord. Together, these women helped carry one another's burdens, encouraged each other, and didn't stop praying until every child was claimed for the Lord. Not only did He change the lives of their children, but He also changed the lives of every mother who was struggling to believe that God's promises are true.

I have seen God work miracles in children's lives. I have seen faithful women pray for years for their children or husbands to return to the Lord and experience His love. I have seen people on their deathbeds turn to God's love, saying that they had a mother or grandmother who had prayed for them for years, and now they finally understood the love of the Lord. If Jesus can forgive a dying man on the cross, saying, "Today you will be with Me in Paradise" (Luke 23:43), He will forgive anyone who earnestly comes to Him at any time. It is possible that our children won't turn to the Lord in our lifetimes. It is also possible that our prayers will result in God bringing more opportunities and more experiences that will direct our children to Him. God does hear the prayers of His people (1 Peter 3:12). Revelation 5:8 tells us that our prayers are like incense before the Lord. They are precious to Him because they reveal our trust and faith in Him. Since we may not know or see all that God does as a result of our prayers, it's important that we trust Him to keep His word.

"If My people who are called by My name will
humble themselves, and pray and seek My face,
and turn from their wicked ways, then I will hear
from heaven, and will forgive their sin and heal their
land. Now My eyes will be open and My ears
attentive to prayer made in this place."
—2 Chronicles 7:14–15

PREPARATIONS ARE OUR RESPONSIBILITY

When the Lord comes to us through a time of prayer, what can we do to prepare our hearts to hear Him? Are there steps we can take? Yes! Scripture gives us many things we can do to keep ourselves ready to hear Him in prayer and respond.

Consistently spending time in God's Word is essential. It is through the Scriptures that we see God's character, His truth, and His guidelines for our daily lives—directions specifically designed to help us know how to have a deeper relationship with Him. As we learn more about the Lord by seeking His truth in Scripture and asking for wisdom and understanding, we will encounter His holiness. He is much more than a friend; He is God. There are times to come into His presence with joy and singing; there are times to come with sorrow in our hearts; there are occasions to come with humility and thanksgiving. If we don't know who God is and what He wants for our lives, it will be impossible to know how to pray. If we don't know what He's said in the Scriptures, we can't be guided by His Word.

At the end of every day, ask the Lord to search your heart to make sure it's clean before Him. If there is unforgiveness, forgive so that God will forgive you (Matthew 6:12). If there is anger or impatience, disobedience, or any other sin that God reveals, ask God to forgive you. He will! Every day, He can set us free from things that can, step by step, take us off of God's path. There is never a wrong time to ask for forgiveness.

Scripture attests to the truth that God often waits on the prayers of His people. Second Chronicles 7:14–15 expresses God's desire to forgive and heal if only His people will return to Him, allow Him to give them a clean heart (by asking forgiveness for their sin), seek after Him, and pray. It is my desire to never make the Lord wait on me, my obedience, or my prayers.

When the disciples asked Jesus to teach them to pray (Luke 11:1), He gave them an amazing and complete answer that continues to guide us today:

"Our Father in heaven, hallowed be Your name. Your kingdom come. Your will be done on earth as it is in heaven. Give us this day our daily bread. And forgive us our debts, as we forgive our debtors. And do not lead us into temptation, but deliver us from the evil one. For Yours is the kingdom and the power and the glory forever. Amen" (Matthew 6:9–13).

And when they had prayed, the place where they were assembled together was shaken; and they were all filled with the Holy Spirit, and they spoke the word of God with boldness.
—Acts 4:31

QUESTIONS FOR DEEPER REFLECTION

1. Scripture and prayer go hand in hand. The more you know about the Lord through His Word, the deeper and more mature your prayer life becomes. As you look at your prayer life over the past few years, can you see your prayers maturing with a greater understanding of how to pray? Has God brought scriptures to mind as you pray? Have you found yourself praying certain verses as you read the Bible? If so, write them down and watch to see how God will answer your prayer. Choose a psalm or a proverb to pray through, asking God to grant you the same promises He has listed in Scripture.

2. Jesus tells us that the Lord honors perseverance and consistency (Mark 7:24–30; Colossians 1:23; Hebrews 3:14; 6:19). Sometimes it is difficult to continue in prayer when there seem to be so few results. It isn't always possible to see God working in another's life. The gentle nudges, the chance meetings of other believers, the teachings from childhood that are brought to mind, the battle waging on the inside—often these are hidden from us. Is there a prayer request you feel God wants you to persevere through and trust Him for? Can He trust you to remain faithful in prayer? Commit to stay the course until you can see the answer, God relieves the burden of the request, or He calls you home.

3. God's timing is always perfect. Sometimes we may not know the circumstances or the reason God has placed someone on

our hearts. When He places a burden on your heart, write it down, pray, and watch to see why the Holy Spirit alerted you to the request.

QUESTIONS FOR GROUP DISCUSSION

1. There are many things we can do to make sure our hearts are right before the Lord. Discuss what some of those things are and what you can do to make sure your lives are clean before the Lord and pleasing to Him.

2. Although God hears the prayers of every one of His children, there is amazing power when we unite in prayer. Are you regularly praying with others? Are you committed to pray until God answers? Share your prayer requests and pray together today. Write down prayer requests and commit to pray for one another this week.

7

ENTRUSTED WITH A CHILD

So God created man in His own image; in the image of God He created him; male and female He created them. Then God blessed them, and God said to them, "Be fruitful and multiply; fill the earth and subdue it."

— Genesis 1:27–28

Why did God choose for us to enter the world so helpless and dependent? What was in His heart when He decided to create the family? From the beginning, God determined that a child would be brought into a family to be cared for, nurtured, loved, and trained in the ways of God. Why did He choose this way? Because He loves us! In giving us children, He provides us with a small glimpse, a picture, of our relationship with Him. It is through His love that He has cared for us, provided for us, trained and often disciplined us, guided us on the right path, and allowed us to be part of His work.

There is an aspect of the Christian life that can only be understood through parenthood. There will be great joys and sorrows, triumphs and tragedies. Through all these experiences, we have the love of the Father and the picture of how He walks with us every day. His expressions of love are our example to follow in all that we do, say, teach, and model for our own children.

And these words which I command you today
shall be in your heart. You shall teach them
diligently to your children, and shall talk of them
when you sit in your house, when you walk by the
way, when you lie down, and when you rise up.
—Deuteronomy 6:6–7

Teaching Until They Learn . . .

One Sunday morning, my well-dressed, scrubbed, and clean five-year-old son was sitting quietly while his Sunday-school teacher was sharing a Bible story with the class. My son was looking at her intently, the epitome of a well-mannered little boy. At the end of the story, the teacher asked if there were any questions. After a few moments, my son raised his hand.

"Yes?" the teacher said, pointing to our sweet child, the pastor's son.

"Mrs. 'Smith'," you're so big and you're so fat, how do you ever fit into the bathtub?"

After a moment of shock at the inappropriate question, she sputtered that this was her concern, and questions should be related to the Bible story. In a matter of minutes, Sunday-school workers were frantically seeking me out to share the tale. Mortified doesn't begin to describe how I felt. Why would he ask such a rude question—at church, nonetheless!

Though embarrassing, this ended up being an important lesson for me: Just because a child is looking at me, being quiet, and seemingly paying attention doesn't mean he's hearing, understanding, or comprehending anything I've said. We can't deceive ourselves that children will learn something simply because we've said it. Teaching isn't a simple process of stating the truth or telling a child how to behave. It is a continuous and challenging process of reviewing and teaching countless times until the information breaks through all the clutter and curiosities the child experiences daily.

Some teachings need years of reinforcement before they are

learned, and this is especially true of biblical principles. Hearing them in church or Sunday school isn't enough for most children. God gave us five senses, and often we must employ each one before we truly understand an important truth. Until you see your child applying a principle you are teaching, don't assume that he or she knows and understands it. Keep teaching!

> *For He established a testimony in Jacob, and appointed a law in Israel, which He commanded our fathers, that they should make them known to their children; that the generation to come might know them, the children who would be born, that they may arise and declare them to their children, that they may set their hope in God, and not forget the works of God, but keep His commandments.*
> —*Psalm 78:5–7*

SHARING THE LOAD

With five children in the house and guests in abundance, there was a never-ending amount of work. So even when the children were small, they were expected to help. There were four areas of service: bathroom, living room, kitchen, and garbage. The kitchen was, by far, the most demanding and dreaded place of service. The kitchen helper was expected to set and clear the table, serve the dessert, make company feel welcome at the table, and help with the dishes. If the helper was lucky, we wouldn't have a lot of company on Sunday—but we almost always did. The living-room helper's responsibility

SUSANNA WESLEY

(1669–1742)

Susanna's world was filled with hardship and struggles. She was the youngest of 25 children, and mother to 19. Tragically, only nine children survived their childhood. Susanna had a heart for the Lord and invested her time and love in her children. She began a household school, where she taught for six hours a day, instilling in each child a deep passion for learning and righteousness.[1] She chose to spend individual time with a different child each evening, investing herself and her faith in her children. Because her husband was often absent, Susanna served as a spiritual guide to her own family.[2] As a means of discipling her children, she began her own Sunday services in her home. Susanna didn't want to deny others the opportunity to learn, so she opened her home, inviting people in the community to attend her services. Eventually, the service grew to more than 200.[3]

Susanna was strict and loving with her children. Although the responsibility of running her household was enormous, she spent two hours each day with the Lord.[4] She had a deep passion for people and their relationship with God. This experience sowed the seeds for the Methodist movement, which would later begin with her sons John and Charles. The Lord honored Susanna's remarkable faith through her children and the sweeping revival He brought about in England called the "Wesleyan Revival."[5]

was to keep it tidy and entertain when we had guests. It was the helper's job to make sure company felt welcome and had enough coffee or tea and to make small talk while I got the refreshments.

Each child took his or her turn for a week at each station. They didn't do their assignments for money or any type of allowance; they did them because they were a part of the family, and with that came responsibilities. Besides, we had no money to give them. Through this process, they learned how to work alongside us, how to clean the house and speak to adults, and the importance of working together as a family. They also learned how to think of others first and put people at ease in social situations.

Lessons of respect and courtesy aren't something we can easily teach a teenager or even an adult, but we can teach them to a child. The responsibility they learned through helping the family, the camaraderie they shared as they teased the "kitchen boy," and being entrusted with specific tasks all shaped our children's characters and helped them mature in their relationship with the Lord. Through each step of obedience to us as they completed their tasks, they were also pleasing the Lord.

All of these lessons were important to us as parents. Teaching my children to help around the house wasn't easy and often took me more time to get things done than if I had done them myself. It required effort! Often, we recognize the importance of teaching spiritual truths to our children but can neglect the practical lessons that are also needed. Our responsibility as parents, though, isn't limited to just teaching our children about spiritual things; our job is to help the Lord shape their character so that He can use them for His purposes.

We also had a responsibility as parents to teach our children manners and social skills so they would be able to succeed in any environment. My mother-in-law always said that any child should be able to eat dinner with the queen and not be uncomfortable because he or she lacked good table manners. Teaching our children responsibility, social skills, protocol, and working together to accomplish a task will help them succeed in every aspect of their lives—in their Christian lives, in their marriages, and in the workplace.

> *Only take heed to yourself, and diligently keep*
> *yourself, lest you forget the things your eyes*
> *have seen, and lest they depart from your heart*
> *all the days of your life. And teach them to*
> *your children and your grandchildren.*
> —Deuteronomy 4:9

Sharing Our Faith

My brother lived in Fort Worth, Texas, while all my boys attended seminary there. He and his wife would often have them over for a meal or for one of my brother's specially baked pies, which they loved. He asked me one day, "If Henry was gone all the time like your kids say, how is it that they know everything he believes about the Lord?" He went on to share that while he was talking to the boys, they would mention that their dad was gone a lot when they were children. Yet in the very next breath they would tell him what their dad believed about this and what their dad said about that.

He was amazed. How could Henry have impressed his faith upon his children as much as he had?

My husband was gone a lot, but he always made an effort to be home for dinner in the evenings, and he was always home for Sunday lunch. At the table, we often talked about our faith or any questions the children had. As the children grew in their own faith, our table became the location of many theological debates. Our guests were often surprised to see how our family interacted. Not only could our children answer difficult questions, but they were also very good at posing them to the unsuspecting!

Family Devotions

Frequently, people ask about the reason all of our children are involved in the ministry in some way. They want to know if this is because of something special we did in our family devotional time. The truth is, for our large family with children in different age groups, family devotions were very difficult. Instead of formal devotions, we took seriously the verses found in Deuteronomy 6:6–7: "And these words which I command you today shall be in your heart. You shall teach them diligently to your children, and shall talk of them when you sit in your house, when you walk by the way, when you lie down, and when you rise up."

When God taught us something, whether it was about our lives or what He was doing through the ministry, we would talk to our children about it. When we sat around the table or drove them to school, as we attended their sports events or watched them play, whenever we were presented with an opportunity for time with our kids, we would talk about the Lord. Any moment throughout the day was a chance to encourage and instruct. Henry also took personal time with each child, asking him or her specific questions that couldn't be answered with a yes or no. It was important for them to learn to think for themselves and know why they believed what they did. Why did Jesus die for you? What difference does that make in your life? How do you know what God wants you to do to be obedient?

Taking our children past the simple answer was important in helping them think for themselves. We knew that our relationship with the Lord wouldn't save them; they had to have their own faith and their own personal relationship with God. Only their own faith would help them when the schools wanted them to participate in reading literature with filthy language; it would help them in the universities, where their professors would mock Christianity and the life of Jesus; it would help them in ministry when they faced painful situations. A vicarious relationship with the Lord wouldn't help our children through life's ups and downs. Only a personal relationship borne of understanding and faith in Christ would carry them through all of life's challenges.

Sports

Encouraging our children to be involved in sports was invaluable. They learned how to obey the coach, how to be disciplined to succeed, how to win and lose equally well, and how to function as part of a team and not just as individuals. When possible, Henry tried to attend the kids' games, whether it was soccer, hockey, or basketball. Once while he watched our two oldest sons' high-school soccer game, a bully, who had been terrorizing several of the younger players, slammed into our second son. Henry knew that our oldest son wouldn't take that lightly. But before Henry could attract his attention, play resumed and our eldest retaliated vigorously. There was clapping from the parents from our team as the referee helped the chastened player back to his feet. This was real life to our kids. Although they were playing a game, they had to make instant decisions and pay the consequences. They had to distinguish right from wrong and deal with difficult situations.

After the game, Henry commended our son for his enthusiasm in protecting his brother but reminded him to be careful how he used his judgment and strength. Henry took advantage of the opportunity to share about God's judgment and justice, and how, as Christians, we can trust Him when someone wrongs us.

When I was a child, I spoke as a child, I understood as a child, I thought as a child; but when I became a man, I put away childish things.
—1 Corinthians 13:11

HELPING OUR CHILDREN GROW

An important aspect of parenting is understanding when to encourage children to do what you know they should do, when you need to motivate them in a special way, and when you must stand back and allow them to do things on their own. This presents great challenges because each child is unique. With five children, I soon learned that the approach I used to help or teach one child wouldn't necessarily work with another.

Giving Our Children a Push

While freezing to death at one of my son's hockey games, I was inspired to encourage the boys to see the value of a wonderful indoor sport: basketball. I knew it was something they would enjoy and succeed at, especially since their father had been a good player in his day, and he could use basketball to spend some time with the boys. I found a team that was enlisting players and signed the three older boys up.

My oldest son wasn't pleased. He offered several excuses: the other kids were younger, he had never played before, and he didn't want to go. He soon realized he was going whether he wanted to or not. I knew this would be a good experience for him, but I literally had to take a broom and sweep him out of the house. He finally decided I wasn't going to change my mind and left with his brothers for practice.

When he came home from that first practice, he had a huge smile on his face. He apologized and then thanked me for making him go. He had a great time and enjoyed the sport. I knew he would be successful, and I was so glad I had stood firmly against my son's opposition. He hadn't wanted to be involved mainly because he didn't know how to play, and he was unsure of himself. This was never a good enough reason in our house, and our children knew they had to try new things. Success wasn't as important as trying and doing one's best.

Motivating Our Children

One of our sons struggled to learn how to read. It had somehow been overlooked at school but became more apparent as he grew older. He was tested and placed with a special teacher, who met with him on a regular basis. She was an exceptional teacher who really sought to help my son succeed.

One day he told me he wanted me to paint something on china for his teacher. A friend and I had been china painting for a few years to help with our finances, and I told my son I would be happy to. However, he had to do something to earn it: He had to work hard for his teacher and try his best.

A few months later, I talked with his teacher to see how he was progressing. She asked if something had happened with my son, because he was working hard and doing well. I realized I needed to start painting! Nothing was working to help him read until he wanted to do something special for his teacher.

Letting Go

My mother once chastised me about how I was raising my daughter. "I can't believe all the things you allow her to do!" was her comment. She wasn't happy. My daughter was named after her, and although my mother never lived near us, she cared deeply for Carrie. At the time, I didn't understand why she was upset, but I didn't dismiss her concerns.

I sought to understand what my mother was saying, and I realized that she thought my daughter should be treated differently from the boys. I had never thought of that. At the time my mother mentioned her concerns, my daughter was driving to Canada from Oklahoma by herself to spend the summer working at her brother's church in Winnipeg. She was 18 and accustomed to driving long distances, as were all my children. I discovered I had raised my daughter to do anything the boys could do, and I didn't try to hold her back, protect her, or place special restrictions on her. It just didn't occur to me.

I trusted Carrie to know what God wanted her to do. I had raised her to be independent, just like the boys. She had to work her way through school, just like the boys. She was allowed to make her own decisions and accept the consequences, just like the boys. When she told me she felt God wanted her to be involved with His work in Bosnia, I swallowed hard and supported her decision. I could do nothing else, as we had raised her to obey the Lord. I believe that God honored my response and her willingness to go by introducing her to her husband and sending them together to a new mission field in Germany, where they serve today.

People often ask how I can live without having any of our children or grandchildren nearby. It's hard for me. What would be more difficult to handle, however, is if they all lived near me but weren't faithful to what God was calling them to do. I would be heartbroken if I knew they hadn't obeyed a call from the Lord because they were worried about me. My husband and I feel honored that God chose to use our children to serve Him; their place of service is up to Him, not us. We raised them in the time God gave us, then we let them go to stand on their own with the Lord and be successful.

Train up a child in the way he should go, and when he is old he will not depart from it.
—Proverbs 22:6

WHEN TROUBLE COMES

There will come a time when our children must grow up, take responsibility, and make decisions on their own. Often, this is when we see all our hard work pay off. We can watch them heed our teaching and stand up for God's truth against opposition or in the face of a crisis. These times will bring the greatest blessings as we see God working in their lives. There is nothing more painful, however, than to watch your children stumble, knowing that they are heading for heartbreak or serious repercussions for their actions. Instead of learning from others' mistakes, many choose to learn the hard way.

One of our children wanted to be different. There came a time in his life when he wasn't walking with the Lord, and it was painful to watch. He didn't enjoy high school, nor would he hear anything about going to college. Learning was a waste of time to him, and he thought that anything he needed to know he could learn in the workplace.

We did everything we knew to draw our son back to the Lord. We didn't hide the fact that there was a problem but asked those around us who loved our family to help. Godly men in the church would take him out to work on cars or speedboats or even take him on white-water rafting trips. My Sunday-school class, which had banded together to pray for our children, was also praying. Our son was always in church, but everything we could think of to do wasn't enough.

One Sunday, when I wasn't playing the organ for the service, I sat in the back of the church. My teenage son arrived late and had to move up a few rows closer to the front—directly in front of me! Every time I looked forward, he was in my line of sight. My heart was so burdened for him. I began to talk to the Lord about him, and as God responded to me, I became quite emotional. The preacher probably thought he was sharing a wonderful and convicting sermon, but I didn't hear a word he said that day. I was too busy listening to what God was telling me.

God reminded me that He loved my child far more than I ever could. What He wanted from me was simple: I needed to take my hands off my son and really give him to the Lord. I had to quit struggling to help him see what he needed to do in his life and allow the Holy Spirit to direct and guide him. If I obeyed, God would take care of him. But at this point, I was in His way.

That was quite a shock for me. For all my efforts, I had actually been hindering the Lord's work in my son's life! Many Kleenexes later, I gave my son to God. It was as if God and our son were on center stage, and Henry and I were backstage. Our job was to love our son and do what the Lord told us to do. We prayed for wisdom and discernment to know where God wanted us to intervene, but we had to allow the Holy Spirit to work in our son's life. I cannot say that everything was easy after this revelation, but God had taken my son out of my hands.

I've been asked many times if I had to give my son over to the Lord again, and if so, how many times. God didn't have to teach me the same lesson twice; once was painful enough! I was often reminded of this lesson, but the issue was settled the day God spoke to me. This one experience with the Lord so impacted my life that I sought to make sure I gave all my children to Him and never stood in His way.

With all of my children, there were struggles and difficulties in which I had to remind myself to allow God to teach them and direct their paths. Having the experience of seeing God work in my children's lives has always brought affirmation and helped me remember that He works in His own way and in His own time. Today, all four boys have earned doctorates from seminary, and each child has chosen to follow the Lord and serve Him.

> *"Whoever receives one of these little children*
> *in My name receives Me; and whoever receives Me,*
> *receives not Me but Him who sent Me."*
> —*Mark 9:37*

"Do-overs"

For many of us, our children are already grown and out of the house. We can never go back and correct mistakes or do things we wish we had done with our children. Yet all is not lost! There are many special ways to continue impacting our children and to have a relationship that brings joy.

Being an example for our children lasts a lifetime. They will continue to watch how we handle sorrows, joys, crises, and challenges. We have a continuing responsibility to encourage them and walk with them through struggles. When they are willing to listen, we can pass on what God has taught us through our relationship with Him. To this day, Henry and I call each of our children to see how they're doing, to ask about what God is doing in their lives, and to share what God is doing in ours. Henry has also written at least one book with each of the children, allowing them to express what we have been trying to teach them throughout their lives, as well as giving Henry the opportunity to share with each as they write.

We try our best to be involved with our grandchildren, even though they live at great distances from us. We continue to pray daily for each of our children and their families. When there are struggles, we pray, and we ask our friends to intercede and stand watch with us until the problem is resolved. As parents of adult children, we can't fix the problems for them anymore. They will make their own decisions and their own mistakes and deal with the consequences themselves. Hopefully, they will never have to question our love and support, and they will always have a place to receive wisdom and encouragement when they need it. The best way to ensure that is for Henry and me to carefully and purposefully walk daily with the Lord.

As we examine our relationship with our children, God may bring to mind some areas in which we could have been more effective, or perhaps He will reveal mistakes we made that impacted our children's lives. Nothing is more healing than sitting down with your child and communicating that you aren't perfect and that you have made mistakes. Sometimes children expect parents to always make the right choices and never have regrets. That just isn't a reality for most of us. Being an example for our children also includes admitting our mistakes and showing them how to deal with situations in a Christlike manner. Whether or not they accept our apology for our mistakes, we have been obedient to what the Lord has placed on our hearts to do.

The righteous man walks in his integrity;
his children are blessed after him.
— *Proverbs 20:7*

TRUSTING GOD WITH OUR CHILDREN

So much of our parenting revolves around our relationship with the Lord. We can't effectively teach something we don't apply to our own lives. When we have an active and growing relationship with the Lord, it's easier to recognize the opportunities God gives us to share with our children. If we're in tune with Him, we're prepared to handle any situation that occurs throughout the day. If we follow His teachings and pass them on to our children, He will bring them to mind when our children face temptations. Henry and I established spiritual markers—reminders of when we had encountered the Lord in our lives and in our family—that helped our children when they had to make important or difficult choices.

As parents, we must teach our children to succeed not only in their relationship with Christ but in their relationships with others. Much of the foundation for success comes from the training they receive as children. We need to take the necessary time to build this into our children. We must methodically plan how we will teach or integrate important principles into their lives. We can't waste time waiting until they are older or until we feel that we have more time to give them. Start now! We will never have a more important job in life than raising the children God has entrusted to us.

Parenting doesn't stop because our children are out of the house; it just takes a different form. We no longer have to teach the dos and don'ts, but we still have the opportunity to show our children the richness of a mature relationship with Christ. Whether they are walking with Jesus or not, our love, patience, grace, and encouragement will make a lasting impact that God can use to influence and change their lives.

QUESTIONS FOR DEEPER REFLECTION

1. If you have children, God has entrusted you with the care and training of your children and commanded you to teach them what the Bible says they are to do. In what ways are you carefully teaching and purposefully instructing your children to succeed both in their spiritual lives and in everyday life?

2. If you're a single person or don't have children, you still have a responsibility to the children God places around you. God chose to place you in certain children's lives to make a difference. Some of the most influential people in the lives of my children have been singles who took time with them, loved them, and helped them grow in Christ. Consider whether God has placed a special child on your heart, and seek ways to encourage and support the child as he or she faces the many challenges of life. Your impact on this child's life will be immeasurable!

3. God is our example in parenthood. His love and care and patience with us are our example to follow as we raise our children. Have you treated and raised your child with the same care and love that God has given to you? Do you use the same patience with your child as God has shown you? The same unending love? The same understanding? Ask God to show you ways you've succeeded and areas that need improvement. Remember that how you treat your child is often the way he or she will one day view the Lord.

4. Many of us will have at least one child who will struggle at some point to follow the Lord. If you've followed all that God has instructed through the Scriptures as you've raised your children, ask Him to help you trust Him as He honors your obedience. Remember, there is no timeframe for God's work! Don't stop praying just because you can't see God's activity. There are infinite ways He can work in your child's life that won't ever be known, quietly drawing him or her to Himself. Every encounter could lead your child into a real and vibrant relationship with the Lord, but it may take time. Be patient and don't stop seeking the Lord on behalf of your children.

Questions for Group Discussion

1. Scripture has a great deal to say regarding how to raise our children. How have you sought to follow the Scriptures in your own families? Share some important lessons you've learned that might help others.

2. God provides daily opportunities to help our children grow spiritually and emotionally. What opportunities has He provided for your children, and how did you react? Discuss some things you are going to do differently to help your children grow in these areas.

3. Has God asked you to let go of your children? Do you sense that He has a special plan for their lives that causes you to fear? Discuss how each of you can let go in a practical way.

8

SEEING THE LIGHT

Being confident of this very thing, that He who has begun a good work in you will complete it until the day of Jesus Christ.
—*Philippians 1:6*

One cold day in Saskatoon, I thought back to my childhood hopes and dreams of seeing the world and living an exciting adventure. I was looking out my kitchen window at the house of one neighbor, who was on a trip to Hawaii. Then I looked over at another house that was closed up for a couple of weeks while the family was on vacation. As I sat pondering, I thought of my sister who was living in Europe and serving as a missionary with her family. My parents were serving in their retirement as missionaries to Africa. How exciting! My reality was that I didn't even have enough money to ride the bus downtown and buy a cup of coffee, much less take a vacation or visit another country. These thoughts were sobering and caused me to think of what my life would have been like if I had made different choices.

As I looked out the window that day, however, I realized that although the other dreams sounded exciting, traveling or living in exciting places wouldn't make me truly happy. My happiness came from being where God wanted me to be and serving Him. In these few minutes of introspection, I told the Lord it was all right if I never experienced my dreams, and I left all my hopes in the Lord's hands. Knowing I was pleasing Him was more important than living in an exotic place or spending money on exciting vacations. I sought to be happy where God had placed me and chose to leave my childhood wishes with Him.

Years later, I discovered that God's plans for my life were so much bigger than my own. When I gave my dreams to the Lord, I truly thought my desire to travel the world would never be fulfilled. I thought we would always remain in Canada. I believed we wouldn't have the financial security others enjoyed. But as I look at what God has done in the past 20 years, I stand amazed at His plans for us. Although I haven't lived in an exotic foreign country, I've now visited about 110 countries! I've also spent a great deal of time with people from around the world, as well as with missionaries who serve with them. Because of my experiences, I have been able to help others who serve in lonely places, who are without family, without money, and sometimes without fellowship or deep friendships. God wanted me to be content in every situation so He could teach me and ready me for the future. He had already prepared tremendous blessings for my life. He had planned to fulfill my hopes and dreams beyond my wildest imagination, but they were still dependent on my obedience and my contentment in my relationship with Him.

> *"But whoever drinks of the water that I shall give him will never thirst. But the water that I shall give him will become in him a fountain of water springing up into everlasting life."*
> —*John 4:14*

WHAT DOES SALVATION MEAN?

I have been asked many times if choosing to be a follower of Christ means giving up things you enjoy—a career, a certain lifestyle, freedom of choice, or habits. Does life become a list of dos and don'ts? Does following Christ consign you to a life of want and sorrow?

The answer lies in understanding why God created us in the first place. We were fashioned to have a relationship with the Lord (Colossians 1:16). We are incomplete without it. Lasting joy and happiness can't be obtained from things or people, for these are temporary and can be gone in an instant. Wealth, health, careers, even family can be taken away or lost. There is nothing on earth that is secure enough to base our lives upon, to trust in completely.

Only in Jesus can we find the never-ending love and security we all seek (Matthew 19:16–22, John 10:10). God's commands are intended to bring peace, happiness, and contentment. The love of money can cause immeasurable heartache, both in a marriage and within the family. A party lifestyle may seem fun at the time, but this behavior is often destructive and potentially dangerous. Even a good job or satisfying career can end in emptiness and disappointment.

Salvation means life and freedom from all the entanglements and pitfalls that lie in every direction. It helps us have a successful marriage as we experience what the true love of Christ is. Raising children isn't a guessing game; God gives us clear guidelines to follow (Deuteronomy 4:9; 6:1–25; Ephesians 6:4). Experiencing the forgiveness of the Lord and the knowledge of His promise to walk with us through the difficult times brings hope.

We weren't created merely to go to heaven when we die; we were made to walk on a daily journey with the Lord here on earth (John 17:13–17). Our time on earth is fleeting, and making use of every moment to know God and to serve Him brings meaning to our lives.

> *Work out your own salvation with fear and trembling;*
> *for it is God who works in you both to will and to*
> *do for His good pleasure. Do all things without*
> *complaining and disputing, that you may become*
> *blameless and harmless, children of God without fault*
> *in the midst of a crooked and perverse generation,*
> *among whom you shine as lights in the world.*
> *—Philippians 2:12–15*

WORK OUT OUR SALVATION . . .

"Salvation is not an event, it is a process."[1] If we want to grow in our Christian walk, it is our responsibility to take an active role in our spiritual growth. Scripture reminds us, "Apply your heart to instruction, and your ears to words of knowledge" (Proverbs 23:12), "listen to counsel and receive instruction" (Proverbs 19:20). Words such as *incline your ear, get wisdom and understanding, apply your heart, cry out for discernment, seek, find,* and *search* all reveal that we must desire a deep

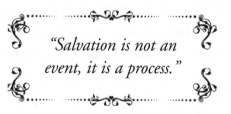

"Salvation is not an event, it is a process."

relationship with God and strive for it. He, in turn, will answer and allow us to experience more of Him. Often, it isn't a burning-bush experience but the quiet voice that daily seeks to guide us toward a deeper walk with Him. God is always working to complete His purposes, and He is looking for someone to love and trust Him enough to follow His voice (Deuteronomy 30:20).

> *The preparations of the heart*
> *belong to man.*
> — *Proverbs 16:1*

God has a purpose for each one of us. He planned our lives from the beginning to experience the fullness of His love, grace, mercy, and joy. All of our experiences are to lead us to know more of God's character and, therefore, to know *Him*. As we grow and mature throughout our lives, as we survive crises, as we grow in our marriages, as we raise our children, we will experience a deeper and more meaningful relationship with the Lord.

Knowing all of this, God entrusts us to work out our own salvation in every area of our lives. He has given us many tools so that we can be successful in our Christian walk. He gave us His Holy Spirit, who helps us understand His words to us. God provided Scripture to guide us in His truth and help us understand His ways and commands for our lives. He has given us direct access to His kingdom and all the power that we need to fulfill His purposes. The Lord has also given us fellowship with His people so we may worship and grow together. And He has provided His presence and His promises to always be with us as we walk with Him.

WITH FEAR AND TREMBLING

When we were told that our daughter had Hodgkin's disease, we were devastated. As her mother, it was heartwrenching to see her endure extremely difficult and painful treatments. One day as I was driving alone, I started telling the Lord all that was on my heart. I didn't know how I could bear this situation. How could I be strong for my daughter when every day was so heartbreaking? I had never faced anything so difficult, and I asked the Lord how I was going to be able to get through it.

The Lord said to me, "I will never leave you, nor forsake you" (Hebrews 13:5). His voice was so clear and vivid that I started looking around to see if the other drivers had heard God's voice too. I had read this scripture a thousand times, but it became so real to me that I knew I wouldn't walk a single step without God's presence with me. It wasn't just a nice thought; it was the answer to my desperate cry.

When God spoke to me that day, He knew I needed to hear from Him. His presence, His holiness, and His power overwhelmed me, and I was literally trembling before Him. He reminded me that nothing was outside of His knowledge or control. This experience gave me much-needed perspective: I had been focusing on my weakness and fear instead of on His power and wisdom. But I didn't have to carry the heavy burden of caring for my daughter alone; I could lean on Him. This brought great freedom and hope to me, and it has been a special experience I've never forgotten.

And when they had prayed, the place where they
were assembled together was shaken; and they
were all filled with the Holy Spirit, and they
spoke the word of God with boldness.
—*Acts 4:31*

When God allows us to experience the fullness of His presence in our lives, we will never be the same. Everything looks different. We want to clearly express our love for Him. Our desire to serve Him with all of our hearts is overwhelming, and we want to stay in His presence while, at the same time, learning and studying to show that we're striving to know Him better. We also want to lay all of our sins at His feet, repenting with great sorrow over our disobedience. God's presence shines a light into our lives, revealing what only He can see.

There is often a misconception regarding "the fear of the Lord." This phrase is found often in Scripture and is linked with the beginning of wisdom (Proverbs 1:7; 9:10; 15:33). The fear of the Lord isn't a negative emotion. It is a truth that protects us from sinning against God (Proverbs 16:6). It is a deep understanding of His power and might.

The apostle Paul, who had an incredible relationship with the Lord, wrote, "Knowing, therefore, the terror of the Lord, we persuade men" (2 Corinthians 5:11). Isaiah, after seeing the Lord sitting on a throne, high and lifted up, said, "Woe is me, for I am undone! Because I am a man of unclean lips, and I dwell in the midst of a people of unclean lips" (Isaiah 6:5). His comments weren't prompted because he was an evil man, for he had already served the Lord for years. But his encounter with the Lord left him so shaken that he could do nothing else but see his shortcomings before God. Experiencing God's presence in a mighty way, seeing a glimpse of who He is in His greatness, and understanding the eternal love He has demonstrated for us provides us with powerful motivation in our Christian walk. Obedience isn't a chore or something we must struggle with and endure; it's our expression to the Lord of our love for Him and because of His great love for us.

The secret of the Lord is with those who fear Him,
and He will show them His covenant.
— Psalm 25:14

A LIFE THAT IS PLEASING

There are so many facets of the Christian walk, and multitudes of applications for our everyday lives. We have only scratched the surface of the many things God wants to teach us. There is always something more to learn, which keeps the Christian walk exciting and fresh. Through many historical and scriptural examples, it is clear that God wants to work in our lives to give us fulfillment and joy. God doesn't love us or call us because of our special talents or abilities. He can provide us with any gifting we need—that isn't difficult for Him! There is no limit to what God can do through us if we love and obey Him.

We cannot possibly know beforehand the journey that the Lord will take us on. Nor can we anticipate all the struggles, successes, difficulties, joys, sorrows, celebrations, heartaches, and triumphs we will experience. That is why our daily walk with the Lord is so important. He has so much to show and teach us, we cannot afford to miss one moment with Him.

One of the benefits to maturing in age is seeing how God brought so many things to completion. His provision and strength have been there for every problem I've encountered. His grace and mercy have always been sufficient for every situation. His wisdom has never been lacking, and His presence has never been far from me. No matter what situation I have dealt with, God has always been there, waiting for me to turn to Him.

God continues to bless our family and challenge us in many new and exciting ways. We never could have foreseen how God would use our ministry throughout the world. We also couldn't have anticipated how God would allow Henry and me to work with our children. Currently, our two oldest boys are working full-time with Blackaby Ministries International. Henry has also spoken at conferences with two of our grandsons. Other members of our family have speaking opportunities through the ministry as well and continue to write about what God is saying to them.

Henry and I have 14 grandchildren, and while we were writing this book, Henry took part in baptizing our youngest granddaughter. It's amazing how our life choices have deeply impacted God's calling on our children and our children's children. There is no room for complacency or relying on previous experiences with the Lord. Something new is always on the horizon! Too much is at stake for us *not* to be walking closely with the Lord every day.

Oh, how great is Your goodness, which You have laid up
for those who fear You, which You have prepared for those
who trust in You in the presence of the sons of men!
—*Psalm 31:19*

GOD KNOWS THE PLANS HE HAS FOR EACH OF US

After Henry and I had spent a number of years in denominational positions, I asked the Lord if He would allow Henry to return to the pastorate. Henry has a loving pastor's heart, and I always enjoyed the challenge of being a pastor's wife. One day God told me that, yes, He could answer my request and allow Henry to return to the pastorate, but He had something else in mind for us. It was as if God was offering me a choice: Did I want Him to grant my request, or did I want God's best for us? Often, God can and does give us what we ask for in prayer, but if we truly want His best, we must trust Him. I'm so glad I chose to trust God's plan for my life instead of insisting on what I thought I wanted. There are so many aspects of the Lord's character I would never have experienced if I had decided to go back to what I knew and loved instead of what He wanted for my life.

Don't settle for anything less than what God has planned for you. Don't allow complacency a foothold in your life that keeps you from becoming all God wants you to be. God has so much in store for you—to give you hope and a future. He only waits on our obedience to Him so He can accomplish His purpose to bring us joy and fulfillment and a life that impacts His kingdom.

*Therefore we also, since we are surrounded by so
great a cloud of witnesses, let us lay aside every
weight, and the sin which so easily ensnares us, and
let us run with endurance the race that is set before
us, looking unto Jesus, the author and finisher of
our faith, who for the joy that was set before Him
endured the cross, despising the shame, and has sat
down at the right hand of the throne of God.*
—Hebrews 12:1–2

AROUND THE KITCHEN TABLE

So many wonderful memories have occurred around my kitchen table—the fun we had at mealtime with the kids, the theological debates, counseling those who were hurting, having coffee with friends, and making donuts and cinnamon rolls. Our kitchen table was the center of our household for many years. It brings back memories of sharing the good and the bad, but especially of seeking to walk together as a family.

This principle of journeying together also applies to us as Christians, as we all walk a similar path in seeking to know the Lord in a deeper and more meaningful way. Our situations, backgrounds, and circumstances may be different, but our desire to love God is the same. When I first started speaking at Experiencing God for Couples weekends, I heard many stories of struggles and disappointments in marriages or in families. Listening to these stories helped me realize that we all have experienced the challenges that life brings. But we aren't alone in our struggles.

Every one of us will encounter difficulties in our lives, but we can support one another and use our combined strength to help each other remain faithful to our Lord. Those of us who have experienced God's faithfulness through the years and have already come through many trials have the privilege of walking with those who are in the middle of their own struggles. Listening to the pain and sharing in the sorrow is sometimes all we can offer one who is hurting. When the crises come there aren't always answers to give—but there are burdens that can be shared.

> *"I know your works. See, I have set before you an open door, and no one can shut it; for you have a little strength, have kept My word, and have not denied My name."*
> *—Revelation 3:8*

WALKING THROUGH THE DOOR

I am incurably curious. I love to meet new people and have new experiences. One reason for this is that God has often surprised me by showing me He was working in some of the most unusual places. My family likes to tease me about having a "bathroom ministry." I can't explain it, but often when I'm at an airport or convention center or some other public place, I meet the most interesting people in the ladies' room! When I enter a restroom or elevator or waiting room, I instinctively say hello to the strangers I meet. I can't tell you how many times the Holy Spirit has used those unexpected encounters to minister to someone.

One day I was in an airport with my husband and oldest son,

and I went to use the restroom. I met a woman who was on her way to visit her daughter and seemed extremely troubled. I asked her if she was okay, and she told me her newlywed daughter had called to say that her husband had just been diagnosed with an advanced case of leukemia, and she was devastated. I led the woman out to where my husband and son were waiting, and with crowds of people swarming all around us, we had a special prayer time with her. I had no idea what I would encounter when I walked through that doorway!

On another occasion, I remember going to help my daughter-in-law Lisa after she had a baby. One day I thought we should walk over to a nearby hamburger place to get a break from her small apartment. Lisa was reluctant to go. My son and his wife were students with very little money, and their apartment was in a dangerous part of town. Next to the hamburger restaurant was a liquor store that was robbed almost every week because it was located by the freeway. My son and daughter-in-law had never gone to this restaurant, even though it was so close to their apartment.

When we entered the restaurant, we saw that it was dirty and dimly lit, and there was hardly anyone sitting at the tables. My daughter-in-law was uncomfortable and suggested we take our food home to eat, where it was safe. But I assured her we'd be okay and could take a moment to eat our food right there. Suddenly, a large bearded man in a leather jacket entered the restaurant. Moments later, he made his way to a table near ours. I could tell that Lisa's worst fears were being realized.

I don't know why God made me such an extrovert, but I just can't help talking to people. So I asked this man what he did for a living. (Judging strictly by appearances, I would have guessed he was a revolutionary—or perhaps a serial killer!) He told us he was a trucker and was passing through town. I asked where he was from, and he replied, "Tulsa."

"Really?" I said. "That's where I grew up!"

To my astonishment, I discovered that he had gone to the same high school I had. We'd even had some of the same teachers. We began to have a delightful conversation. This lonely, hurting man had obviously had no one to talk to for some time. When we finally left, he gave us a hearty good-bye, and we parted as new friends. (My daughter-in-law has told that story countless times since.)

What I have come to realize is that when you choose to walk with the Lord, every day is a new adventure. Life may be difficult and come with challenges, but with God, *all* things are possible! Every time I see a door, I wonder, *What does God have in store for me behind that door?* Is it a hurting mother wanting to know why God would allow her young son-in-law to develop leukemia? Is it a lonely trucker wondering if there is anyone who cares about him? There are so many people who need to know that with God there is always hope, and with Christ forgiveness is always available.

Sadly, some Christians stand outside the doors set before them and are afraid to enter. Fear, doubt, insecurity, and past failures all cause people to be too afraid to move forward with God. I don't know about you, but I don't want to get to the end of my life and wonder what it would have been like if I had trusted God enough to walk through the open door He had set before me. At times, you will have no idea what will happen if you trust God and do what He tells you. But after years of walking through those open doors with God, I can assure you, it's always worth it. As I've said before, living life for and with God is always an adventure! Is that how you would describe your life?

God has a purpose for every one of His children. He won't reveal His complete plan in the beginning, but He will show us each step we need to take to grow in our relationship with Him. We need to constantly evaluate our lives.

Are you learning something new about the Lord each time you open His Word? Do you anticipate that when you open the Bible, God will reveal Himself and expect you to adjust your life and follow Him in obedience? Is it possible that you have coasted on past successes in your life and haven't had a fresh encounter with the Lord in a long time?

God wants to show us something new every day. He wants to work through our lives to grow His kingdom. If growing in your Christian walk is your deepest desire, you will be able to describe your life as David did in Psalm 1: "He shall be like a tree planted by the rivers of water, that brings forth its fruit in its season, whose leaf also shall not wither; and whatever he does shall prosper" (verse 3).

If you are a child of God, and you have chosen to make Him Lord of your life, He will take every opportunity to draw you closer to Him, to help you grow, and to help you experience more of His amazing love for you. Expect that He will work through your life to fulfill His purpose. God could open your heart to be the "block mom" that the kids can trust and seek advice from. God may want your life to impact those around you in the workplace. God could ask you to be involved in missions in some way—either locally or internationally. He may want you to teach a Bible study or lead

Sunday school, to bake cookies for the kids and take the time to see how God is moving in their lives, to seek to be a Christian influence at work and in your neighborhood, or to pray for and encourage a friend. There are no small assignments in God's kingdom! Look for how He is daily working through your life, and He will show you great and amazing things beyond anything you could ever ask or imagine.

QUESTIONS FOR DEEPER REFLECTION

1. When was the last time you had a powerful sense of God's presence when you turned your attention to Him? Did you experience the awe and wonder that comes with the knowledge of who God is? Have you ever trembled before God, knowing that He holds the universe in His hand? If not, you're missing a vital part of your Christian life. Ask God to reveal Himself to you in a fresh and powerful way—and then wait until He does it!

2. Working out our salvation is a great gift the Lord has given us. How have you treated that gift? We're accountable for how we choose to work out our salvation. Consider what this means for you personally. Make the choice to strive, earnestly seek, search, acquire, get, study, labor, obtain, and find the wisdom and knowledge of the Lord—which leads to abundant life.

3. We all have hopes and dreams of where we would like to be and what we would like to do. But sometimes dreams can stand in the way of our obedience to the Lord. What are your

dreams for your life or the lives of your family? Are there any dreams you hold so tightly that you aren't willing to give to the Lord? How can you begin to let go of your dreams and let God make them come true in His way, in His timing, and as a deep expression of His love for you?

QUESTIONS FOR GROUP DISCUSSION

1. Did you have hopes and dreams as a child? If so, what were they? Has God allowed any of your dreams to be fulfilled? Has God changed your dreams beyond the scope of your imagination? Please explain.

2. With our salvation comes freedom from all the entanglements of sin in our lives. If you are a follower of Christ, has your life been a list of dos and don'ts, or have you been living in freedom by following God's path for your life? What does the difference mean to you?

3. When you think of the phrase "fear of the Lord," how have you understood its meaning in the context of Scripture? Is fear of a holy God negative? Has your understanding of this important Scriptural truth deepened? Please explain.

4. God presents us with so many opportunities each day. Are you ready to experience the fullness of Christ in your life? Are you ready to open the door and see what God has for you? Share some of the opportunities God has given you recently and how you have responded to them.

NOTES

Chapter 1

1. We highly recommend Madame Guyon's book *Experiencing God Through Prayer* (New Kensington, PA: Whitaker House, 1984), arranged and revised by Donna C. Arthur.
2. Edith Deen, *Great Women of the Christian Faith* (Chappaqua, NY: Christian Herald Books, 1959), 130-40.

Chapter 2

1. Henry Blackaby and Carrie Blackaby Webb, *Prepared to Be God's Vessel* (Nashville: Thomas Nelson Publishing, 2006).
2. Ruth A. Tucker and Walter L. Liefeld, *Daughters of the Church* (Grand Rapids, MI: Zondervan, 1987), 308.
3. Edith Deen, *Great Women of the Christian Faith* (Chappaqua, NY: Christian Herald Books, 1959), 248.
4. Ibid., 249.
5. Ibid., 252.
6. Ibid., 249.
7. Ibid., 247-54.

Chapter 3

1. Edith Deen, *Great Women of the Christian Faith* (Chappaqua, NY: Christian Herald Books, 1959), 243.
2. Ibid., 240-46.

3. George Müller, quoted in Henry Blackaby, Richard Blackaby, and Claude King, *Experiencing God: Knowing and Doing the Will of God,* rev. ed. (Nashville: LifeWay Press, 2007), 40.

Chapter 4

1. Edith Deen, *Great Women of the Christian Faith* (Chappaqua, NY: Christian Herald Books, 1959), 94.
2. Ibid., 92.
3. Ibid., 96.

Chapter 5

1. Edith Deen, *Great Women of the Christian Faith* (Chappaqua, NY: Christian Herald Books, 1959), 385.
2. Ibid.
3. Ibid.
4. Ibid.

Chapter 6

1. Andrew Murray, *Andrew Murray Devotional* (New Kensington, PA: Whitaker House, 2006), 19.
2. Bertha Smith, as quoted in Timothy and Denise George, eds., *Bertha Smith: Go Home and Tell* (Nashville: Broadman & Holman, 1995), 196.
3. Ibid., 23.
4. Ibid., 39.

Chapter 7

1. Edith Deen, *Great Women of the Christian Faith* (Chappaqua, NY: Christian Herald Books, 1959), 143.
2. Ruth A. Tucker and Walter L. Liefeld, *Daughters of the Church* (Grand Rapids, MI: Zondervan, 1987), 237.
3. Ibid., 238.
4. Deen, 142.
5. H. Leon McBeth, *The Baptist Heritage* (Nashville: Broadman Press, 1987), 151.

Chapter 8

1. Henry T. Blackaby and Richard Blackaby, *Experiencing God Day by Day* (Nashville: Broadman & Holman, 1998), 205.

ABOUT THE AUTHORS

MARILYNN SUE BLACKABY is the wife of Henry Blackaby, author of *Experiencing God.* Marilynn has been a pastor's wife for 30 years and is a much sought-after speaker on the difference God can make in your everyday life. She has led many women's retreats and Experiencing God for Couples conferences, and she has a deep passion for helping people understand the love of the Lord. For her efforts in counseling and encouraging others, she was given an honorary doctor of discipleship from California Baptist University, where she also earned her bachelor's degree. Currently, along with traveling and speaking with her husband, Marilynn serves as the business manager for Blackaby Ministries International. She is the mother of five children, who have all dedicated their lives to the Lord's service. She is also delighted to be the grandmother of 14 grandchildren.

CARRIE BLACKABY WEBB is the coauthor of *Prepared to Be God's Vessel: Lessons from the Life of Mary* and is the youngest child of Henry and Marilynn Blackaby. Carrie earned a master's of divinity degree from Southwestern Baptist Theological Seminary and a bachelor of music degree from Oklahoma Baptist University. She has worked on staff in several churches in the areas of music and worship, children's ministry, and youth work. She has been a speaker for various missions conferences and shares with women's groups. For the past eight years, Carrie and her husband, Wendell, have served as career missionaries in Germany, as team leaders and strategy coordinators for the Hochsauerland region. They have two children, Elizabeth and Joshua.

Blackaby Ministries *(www.blackaby.org)* was established to respond to increasing opportunities for ministry globally. The key ministries that make up Blackaby Ministries International:

- Marketplace Ministry
- Writing Articles
- Training Institute
- International Conferences
- Preaching / Teaching / Speaking

The heart-cry of the Blackaby family is to disciple God's people in such a way that God's Holy Spirit would bring revival in the hearts of God's people and spiritual awakening to a lost world.

FOCUS ON THE FAMILY®

Welcome to the family!

Whether you purchased this book, borrowed it, or received it as a gift, we're glad you're reading it. It's just one of the many helpful, encouraging, and biblically based resources produced by Focus on the Family for people in all stages of life.

Focus began in 1977 with the vision of one man, Dr. James Dobson, a licensed psychologist and author of numerous best-selling books on marriage, parenting, and family. Alarmed by the societal, political, and economic pressures that were threatening the existence of the American family, Dr. Dobson founded Focus on the Family with one employee and a once-a-week radio broadcast aired on 36 stations.

Now an international organization reaching millions of people daily, Focus on the Family is dedicated to preserving values and strengthening and encouraging families through the life-changing message of Jesus Christ.

Focus on the Family Magazines

These faith-building, character-developing publications address the interests, issues, concerns, and challenges faced by every member of your family from preschool through the senior years.

Focus on the Family **Citizen®** U.S. news issues | Focus on the Family **Clubhouse Jr.™** Ages 4 to 8 | Focus on the Family **Clubhouse™** Ages 8 to 12 | **Breakaway®** Teen guys | **Brio®** Teen girls 12 to 16 | **Brio & Beyond®** Teen girls 16 to 19 | **Plugged In®** Reviews movies, music, TV

FOR MORE INFORMATION

 Online:
Log on to www.family.org
In Canada, log on to www.focusonthefamily.ca

 Phone:
Call toll free: (800) A-FAMILY (232-6459)
In Canada, call toll free: (800) 661-9800

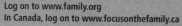

BP06XFM

More Great Resources
from Focus on the Family®

Blessing Your Husband
Debra Evans

Do you long for a closer relationship with your husband? To understand him more and discover the depths of his soul? Try something new—start blessing him. As you read *Blessing Your Husband*, you'll discover the undeniable influence your thoughts, words, attitudes, and actions have on the man you married. Blessing your husband conveys your approval of him, thereby confirming that he is lovable, capable, and valuable, simply because of who he is. You'll be amazed at how something so simple can transform your marriage, your outlook, and your life.

Closer: Mother & Daughter—Closer to God and to Each Other
Susie Shellenberger

Take one part talking, two parts listening, sprinkle liberally with Scripture and fun activities, and what do you have? Susie Shellenberger's book *Closer*. Written especially for mothers and teen daughters, *Closer* is designed to help moms and daughters share their hearts and grow closer together.

Beyond the Masquerade
Dr. Julianna Slattery

Today's Christian women are under more pressure than ever before. They so desperately want to play the part of the ideal wife, mother, and church-goer that they often wear "masks" to protect themselves from the world's impossible standards. These masks separate us from God, from each other, and from our true selves. Thankfully, there is hope beyond the masquerade. This book reveals how Christ can heal and transform our lives, freeing us from bondage. *Beyond the Masquerade* calls women to live life abundantly—as God intended!

FOR MORE INFORMATION

 Online:
Log on to www.family.org
In Canada, log on to www.focusonthefamily.ca.

 Phone:
Call toll free: (800) A-FAMILY
In Canada, call toll free: (800) 661-9800.

BP06XP1